The Enlightenment Workbook
of Buddhist Mysticism

Samvara

Written in gratitude for my teacher
And dedicated to the Enlightenment of you

Contents

The Truth _____ 1

Stories _____ 2

Realization Is the Goal _____ 7

The Buddha's Story _____ 12

Learning from the Buddha Now _____ 16

What Is Buddhism? _____ 17

Buddhist Stories _____ 20

    The Story of the Wheel of Life _____ 23

    The Story of Reincarnation _____ 26

    The Story of Karma _____ 26

The Adventure Begins! _____ 29

The First Noble Truth _____ 31

    The Suffering of Pain _____ 32

    Change Brings Death _____ 42

    Finding Peace in Death _____ 43

    Death Stories _____ 45

    The Truth about Death _____ 52

    The Conclusion of Suffering _____ 53

The Second Noble Truth _____ 54

    Good and Bad Are Ugly _____ 56

    Desires Are Endless _____ 60

    Wherever You Go, There You Are _____ 63

    The End of Desire _____ 66

    Fear _____ 67

The Third Noble Truth _____ 75

The Fourth Noble Truth _____ 77

    Right Meditation _____ 78

    Right Mindfulness _____ 84

    Right View _____ 88

    Right Intent _____ 93

    Right Speech _____ 97

    Right Action _____ 101

    Passions, Should-Do's, and Right Action _____ 104

    Society's Dream and Right Action _____ 106

    Right Action in Motion _____ 108

    Right Job _____ 110

    Right Effort _____ 115

Buddhism's Result: Freedom _____ 119

Mystical Teachings _____ 131

What Is Power? _____ 134

Responsibility _____ 137

Enjoy the Process! _____ 139

The Use of Power for Evolution _____ 141

Proof that You're Psychic _____ 143

The Past Is Dust _____ 145

Healing Emotional Sores by Changing the Past _____ 150

Relationships _____ 155

The Transient Lifecycle of Relationships _____ 156

Taking Stock of Your Power_____ 159

Taking Stock of Your Relationships _____ 165

Power Plan_____ 167

Penny for Your Thoughts _____ 174

Ordering the Chaos of the Mind _____ 183

Mystical Fashion _____ 185

Mystical Exercises _____ 190

Selfless for Yourself _____ 193

Conclusion_____ 197

A True Story_____ 200

The Truth

Enlightenment is the complete awareness of life. It is absolute consciousness unlimited by the fears, desires, and conceptual models of the self. This freedom can only be described as ecstasy.

Enlightenment is the union of all things. It is the intimate connection of the finite and infinite, of the surface and essence, of the physical and spiritual. This unbound harmony can only be described as love.

Enlightenment is blissful liberation from suffering. It is the absence of a grasping, fearing, and controlling self. This nonexistence can only be described as peace.

Stories

The "Big Picture" is important to all of us, yet most of us don't really know a whole lot about the Big Picture. "Who am I and why am I here?" "What's the meaning of life?" "Does god exist?" "Is there an afterlife?" To answer these questions, we predominantly rely on old religious stories, but have very little firsthand information. Although our understanding is limited, the truth about life is important to us because of the inevitable fact that someday we will die.

Religions are like languages describing the story of truth in different ways. Many religions are rooted in truth. The saints and prophets who had inspired these faiths saw the Big Picture and taught the whole truth. Decades or even centuries later, self-appointed custodians structured, codified, and organized the words and teachings of the founding saints into the forms of religion that we see today.

Though custodians have studied their founders' teachings, the custodians' direct awareness of the Big Picture often falls short from that of their founder. The difference lies in the fact that custodians interpret the words of truth taught by their founder, while the founder's words were expressions of truth spoken by someone who saw the Big Picture. It's not hard to see that the wisdom you would gain from being directly taught by Jesus would likely be far greater than the wisdom you would gain attending your local preacher's sermons.

Veiled over time by custodial interpretation, the teachings of the founders of religion have become overlain with extraneous information. These teachings that once brought liberation are now shrouded in obscuration and mired in ambiguity. The spiritual essence of these teachings has become almost completely lost, and the Big Picture understandings that most people get from organized religion in the end bring little peace of mind.

Science gives us Big Picture stories too. In modern times science has emerged as a powerful influence on the way we see life. Scientific views of reality have conditioned our awareness as a society and have elevated our views of life so that it is difficult for us to buy into the stories, cosmologies, and religions of the past. It's not realistic to us that god made the Earth in six days. We all know that's not what they say on the Discovery Channel! The religious story descriptions of god, heaven, and hell don't grip us now as they gripped people a thousand or a hundred years ago.

Yet the scientific mindset has not elevated our consciousness enough to account for some of the most essential dimensions of life, such as love. So, although we know more things, we feel more alienated by them, alone in a vast, impersonal and meaningless universe. We understand the objects, structures, and mechanics of the universe, but have lost our place in the universe, our connection to all things.

Society also tells us stories. Society's stories tell us who we are and what will make us happy. Society's stories are often more compelling than scientific and religious stories because, while narrower in scope, they have a lot more to do with our day-to-day lives.

Society has a compelling plan for us based on general parameters such as our gender, our income bracket, and the color of our skin. With these criteria society dictates to us an authoritative story that tells us who we are. The societal self-definition has tremendous weight because it is reflected back to us and reinforced every time we shop, dine out, watch TV, read magazines, work, or go to school.

The problem is that this definition of self is greatly limited. Society lumps each of us into a demographic with at least a million other people and holds us to the perception of that group's most common societal attributes. Society's definition of self robs us of our individuality, uniqueness, and spiritual independence.

Society also tells us a powerful story of what is "good," what is "bad," and what will make us "happy." Society tells us that success and beauty are good. Society informs us that success comes from having a high paying job and an accumulation of fine objects. Society describes beauty as being tall, thin, and fair-skinned.

Society cautions us that being different is bad. Society conditions us to fit in to the mold of a proper "lady" or "gentleman." Society warns us not to speak, dress, or act differently from societal norms.

Finally, society teaches us that happiness comes from having a relationship with a proper lady or gentleman who is successful and beautiful. In the United States our societal story of happiness is called the American Dream. The American Dream tells us that happiness is having a house with a white picket fence, a successful and beautiful spouse, 2.3 children, and a Ford parked in the driveway.

We, modern day Westerners with more civil rights and choices than ever, have heard many stories of faith and fact that describe life. We have had so many stories marketed to us that we don't really know which ones to buy into. The contradictions amongst the stories only serve to confuse us further.

We are more open-minded than ever, but also more apathetic. It's hard to swallow religious stories on faith when they don't match our reality. The things we learn in church often have little to do with our experiences in school and the working world. At the same time, it's hard to believe that the American Dream is enough. The stories society and the media tell us are often more meaningful to our experience than those of the church, but they offer no lasting satisfaction.

Amid all of the stories, it plays out that most people shelve the distant religious Big Picture stories as abstract concepts and choose stories that are more self-serving in the short term as reality. Most people don't follow the spirit of their religion; they follow the spirit of *stuff-ism*. Stuff-ism is a synthesis of the scientific "object and mechanism reality" story and the social "this is happiness" story. Stuff-ism essentially comes down to seeking happiness by getting ...stuff.

Most people seek happiness through acquisition. They think that they will be happy if they can get enough money, power, and respect. They think that if only they can get the right relationship, the perfect family, the dream house, the right job, the right car, the right cell phone, and the right ...stuff, that they will find fulfillment.

But even as we engage in the drama of seeking stuff from life's cornucopia of stuff we all want, we are at the same time painfully aware that one day we will die and that there isn't any stuff that will ultimately fulfill us and bring us eternal peace. The threat of this imminent death sentence reminds us that when the stuff hits the fan, you can't take the stuff with you!

The good news is that there *is* a way for you to be truly happy in this seemingly crazy world. There is a way to eternal peace. There is a way to ultimate fulfillment. There is a way to move beyond the trappings of a life where we can't believe the old stories, yet the new reality leads us to no satisfaction. The way is Enlightenment. It is to experience life directly and completely, beyond limited stories.

Life itself is complete truth. Stories are partial truths. What a story can't express is what makes it incomplete. Religious stories are partial truths, limited by custodial interpretation, and lacking relevance due to a social and historical disconnect from our daily experience. Scientific stories are partial truths, unable to express essential dimensions of life such as love and happiness. Societal stories are partial truths, unable to express eternity.

The complete truth cannot be contained in words. If someone told you a story about the ocean, but you had never swum in the ocean, sailed on the ocean, or even seen the ocean, then what would you know about the ocean? You would know a conceptual and partial truth that pales in comparison to the actual truth.

Many of us know about the ocean. We know about its waves, tides, and currents. We know of its fish and mammals, its corals and sponges. We know how to swim in the ocean and stay safe from drowning. The stories we have about the ocean give us important information for our health, well being, and enjoyment of the ocean, but if we understood the ocean to be only this information, we would be cutting ourselves off from the most essential awareness of the ocean: the awareness of the ocean's spirit. Yet if we would look deeper, beyond all surface information, we would become aware of the ocean's infinite spiritual essence.

Most people interact with life largely at a conceptual level, unconnected to a deeper awareness of life beyond surface views. They have stories and ideas about life and interact with life through these perfunctory views without apprehending life's greater dimensionality, life's spirit.

The mind is conditioned through stories for understanding life. These stories are frozen conceptual models that help us understand things in a limited way, but ultimately block us from seeing the deeper truths of reality.

It is as if your mind were a clear glass of pure water. The truth is like sunlight, illuminating the center of the body of water. The stories we're told start to freeze our fluid minds into rigid forms. As the water freezes, our naturally clear mind becomes solid and opaque. We can no longer see sunlight in the water. The light is reflected and refracted on the surface while the heart of our mind becomes unilluminated.

The Enlightenment Workbook is filled with stories! This book conveys to you new frozen concepts that will crack open the rigid concepts that you've had for years to show you that there really is a Big Picture of truth beyond what you've always thought.

From a close-minded perspective, you can find fault with all words, teachings, and stories. As soon as words are used, a bias forms. As soon as words are interpreted, additional bias may be assumed. All stories have bias and can be construed in positive or negative ways. This bias is evident when different people or groups quote *The Bible* to support anything from selfless giving to racism.

Yet just as Rama Krishna, an Enlightened teacher of India would say, "You remove the thorn that inflicts you by using another thorn as the instrument to end the suffering." This book uses stories and concepts to show you the truth beyond stories and concepts.

Gautama Buddha, an Enlightened teacher of ancient India and the founder of Buddhism, taught the path to the complete awareness of life. He taught attention to the direct perception of life, seeing life as it is in its endless dimensions. Buddha taught that awareness and experience are the pathway to

Enlightenment. Buddha's teachings are direct and practical. They illuminate the truth of life and foster awakening in the awareness of your own experience.

Your own experience therefore is the true story. Your awareness of life contains all of the answers for the Big Picture questions while being completely relevant to what will make you happy now. Though the stories that others tell you are partial truths, your story is your whole experience of life. Your experience of life is complete truth. Complete truth exists right now in your own experience!

Yet reflect on your awareness of life up to this moment. How complete is your awareness of your experience? Consider that you are like the ocean, deep and vast. Beneath the surface, you contain a universe of intricacy and possibility. Do you know your whole story yet? Have you considered all of who you are?

The Enlightenment Workbook will guide you to recollect all aspects of yourself and your experience, so that you can reach a new and complete awareness of life. Following the Buddha's teachings, you will discover your unique pathway to Enlightenment, your true story.

Realization Is the Goal

The goal of this book is to bring you to two bona fide spiritual realizations! The first realization is that Buddha's teachings work. This realization awakens you to see how Buddha's teachings are alive and useful in your own experience of life. The second realization is the realization of power. This realization yields a mystical awareness of an Enlightened power. Once aware of this power, you can use it for evolution and greater happiness in your life. This power helps you apprehend positive opportunities and aids you in overcoming obstacles to your success.

The Enlightenment Workbook then is not just a book that gives you conventional knowledge. This is a magical book. This book is Buddhist mysticism for your Enlightenment. This book brings you into a greater awareness of life. This book guides you through mystical means to directly point to your own mind, so that you can see the truth.

The Enlightenment Workbook will bring you to a higher awareness. You will soar high up above your usual state of attention. You will be able to see your life in new ways that open opportunities for greater happiness. It is as if you were driving down a highway on a long trip, and suddenly you were elevated up thousands of feet above the highway. High up in the sky you can see for miles all around you! You can see beyond the limits and barriers of your usual perceptual position.

You can see where the highway leads and if there are any traffic jams or road blocks ahead. You can see other routes and roads that you could not see or consider as possibilities from the ground. You are also able to see different destinations and understand your journey better.

You might be wondering why this book is called a Workbook. Doing the Enlightenment Workbook is an active exploration of self. Work, or purposeful activity, is an effective method of self-discovery.

In this book you will be given tasks and writing assignments. Do not merely read the Enlightenment Workbook. This book demands your full attention. The Enlightenment Workbook offers wisdom and realization, but only if you follow the directions for the assignments carefully and do them to the best of your ability with a great degree of self-honesty.

If you do not follow the directions of the Enlightenment Workbook, you will simply gain some new information that will ultimately only serve your egotism and ignorance. The Buddha said, "The fool cleaves his own head with the knowledge he accumulates."

Rule #1 for the Enlightenment Workbook is that you don't skip steps or fake it. Rule #2 for the Enlightenment Workbook is that you don't skip steps or fake it. Only study the Enlightenment Workbook if you are following both rules.

It is extremely important that you follow the instructions, do the assignments, and do them in sequential order. Be honest. Reflect deeply and be true. No one is grading your assignments. To succeed with this book you don't have to be clever or interesting, you just have to do the work and be honest.

In the Far East people don't start a spiritual study unless they've already committed themselves to learning its essence. In the West we like to try a little of this and a little of that, to see what things are like. This way, we become a jack of all trades, but master of none. In contrast, the wisdom of the Orient tells us that if we master one thing, we will know the essence of all things.

Do you know anyone who has taken a karate class? Many people have had an interest in learning the power of martial arts. Most of them have studied for a couple weeks, a few months, or up to a year. They tried it out, got a yellow belt, figured that they got the idea of what martial arts is, but decided that it was a bit too hard, too long, too time-consuming, and that they had other things to do.

How many people do you know who have a black belt? How many people took the art to a point of mastery? These are serious students. They didn't just get an introduction to the art. They didn't try to skip steps. They learned it. They did it. They have the power to defend their lives and the lives of others with mastery.

Just as there's no faking it in defending your life from physical harm, there's no faking it in being Enlightened, happy, or at peace. There are no skipping steps in life. Everything you learn about life, every spiritual truth gained, must be learned by heart.

You can, however, learn quickly when you bring your best to the task. So put your heart into it as you quest for the awakening of spirit through the Enlightenment Workbook!

This book is an adventure! The Enlightenment Workbook sets you on a spiritual exploration of awareness in the frontiers of your own mind.

Assignment: My Enlightenment Journal

Now it is time for your first assignment. Buy an Enlightenment Journal. An Enlightenment Journal is a blank book. It is a memoir where you will write your reflections and experiences for the assignments during the study of the Enlightenment Workbook. Do not use a notebook that you already have. Go to a store and buy a new one.

Your Enlightenment Journal does not have to be fancy, but it will be an important part of your life for the next couple of months, so quality and aesthetics are beneficial.

Depending on your writing style and how large your penmanship is, your Enlightenment Journal can easily end up being over 100 pages. If you reach the end of your Enlightenment Journal before completing this study, simply buy a new Enlightenment Journal and continue.

Upon getting your Enlightenment Journal, entitle the first page, "(*enter your first and last name*)'s Enlightenment Journal" in large letters.

Turn the page. Entitle the second page, "What I want to know." What answers are you seeking in life? Reflect for a moment on what you want to know. Write down what you hope to learn by doing the Enlightenment Workbook. List what you want to know in your Enlightenment Journal.

It's OK if you want to know just one thing and it's OK if you want to know many things. It's OK to list statements or questions. Whatever it is about life, Enlightenment, and the Big Picture that you want to know, list it now.

If you do the assignments in the Enlightenment Workbook to the best of your ability and in the spirit of the instructions, you may just find out what you want to know.

Complete this assignment now. Continue reading when finished.

Post Assignment

If you did your assignment correctly, you went to the store to buy a new Enlightenment Journal. The magic in this lesson is in going to the store! Action is important in mysticism. Funny actions that don't seem connected or important sometimes are the most vital for shifting your awareness.

In my old martial arts school I wanted to learn to kick and punch just like the action stars I saw in the movies. My sensei, or martial arts teacher, said that if I wanted to learn the essence of the art I should learn to stand instead of learning to kick and punch. He taught me only stances for the first year. It was hard, painful, and boring. Though I didn't understand why I had to do stance training, I did it because I really wanted to learn martial arts.

It was ten years later that I came to understand why standing is more important than striking in martial arts. Stance is balance. For martial artists balance is the foundation of power. Punches and kicks are completely ineffective without balance. If you have balance, any attack or defense has power.

Do not try to skip steps. Take it nice and slow. If you did not complete the assignment properly, redo the assignment correctly. The magic of going to the store to buy your Enlightenment Journal will reveal its value in time as a means of bringing balance.

Assignment: The Stories of My Life

Entitle a new page in your Enlightenment Journal, "The Stories of My Life."

Write a summarized version of your life story. This is not an exhaustive recapitulation of your life. Just recall the important events, relationships, and experiences and what they mean to you.

To write your life story, briefly describe the following:

1. How do your defining qualities affect your life?
   a. Ethnicity
   b. Spirituality, religion, and faith
   c. Gender and sexuality
   d. Education and occupation
   e. Hobbies and interests
   f. Strengths and weaknesses
2. What's your family like?
3. How was your childhood?
4. Have you ever been in love?
5. What have your relationships with your friends been like?
6. Who or what have been your greatest influences (good and bad)?
7. What were the three most important events of your life?
8. What challenges have you faced in life?
9. What have you learned about life?
10. What makes you happy?
11. What really matters to you?
12. What's the Big Picture story that you really believe?

Complete this assignment now. Continue reading when finished.

The Buddha's Story

Now let's consider the story of the Buddha. Let's see who he was and what he learned. Before the Buddha was called the Buddha, his birth name was Siddhartha. Over 2500 years ago, Siddhartha was born in northern India at the foothills of the Himalayas.

When Siddhartha was born, his father, the king of the land, sought the insight of an old sage wise in astrology to determine the proper path for his son to lead in life. The sage foretold that Siddhartha could succeed in two routes. The first route was as an Avatar, an Enlightened teacher. The second route was as a great king. Siddhartha's father wished for Siddhartha to be a great king and heir to the throne. Furthermore, he feared that if his son followed a spiritual path that he would be separated from him. So, Siddhartha's father decided that he would teach his son only the path of a great monarch.

Siddhartha was raised in luxurious palaces, wearing silk robes, eating the finest foods, with servants and beautiful courtesans. He excelled in his academic studies, in archery, and in horsemanship. Siddhartha's father grew proud and happy with the path his son was on. Siddhartha grew up content and proud. As a young man he married a beautiful princess who gave birth to their son. He had everything he could ever want and lived in great comfort.

All seemed perfect until a nagging feeling arose in Siddhartha. Despite his comfortable and luxurious life, Siddhartha started to feel as though something was missing, as if his heart was empty. He felt as if he were asleep and expected to wake up.

Siddhartha had no way to explain, understand, or express his heart's dissatisfaction until one day, the song of a courtesan caught his attention. Many of the subjects in his court played musical instruments and sang songs, but this woman's song was somehow different. The melody of her stringed instrument was powerful and ancient. Her voice rang with deep sorrow and strength. Siddhartha was moved to tears. He found in her song the doorway out of his sorrow. Her music was an expression of his heart.

Siddhartha's father was upset to see his grown son crying. He ushered a servant to help Siddhartha. Upon the servant's inquiry into Siddhartha's ailment, Siddhartha asked about the origin of the woman's song. The servant explained that it was the song from another land, that it was a song about a spiritual place in the Himalayas.

The power and magic of music forever changed Siddhartha's life at that moment. His spirit was ignited. He wondered where this spiritual place could be. He had never seen a holy place. He had never even seen his own kingdom. He decided he must go out of the palace and see the world beyond the walls that confined him.

Siddhartha's father was very displeased and resisted Siddhartha's request to venture out of the safety of the palace, but Siddhartha insisted that he needed to see what was beyond the palace walls. Reluctantly agreeing, his father devised a plan. He ordered a parade. The streets were decorated and lined with young and beautiful people adorned in silk clothing. His father made the streets look much like the palace. So it was that during the parade Siddhartha saw a beautiful city filled with young, beautiful subjects.

As his initial excitement began to fade, Siddhartha noticed two odd-looking, short men walking down a narrow street. Siddhartha abruptly ended his procession, dismounted his elephant, and pushed his way through the crowds toward the two men despite the pleas of his servants to return. Upon reaching the two men, Siddhartha noticed that they were wrinkled and hunched over. Here Siddhartha learned about old age. Siddhartha followed the two old men and came across another old man, who was gravely ill. Here Siddhartha learned about illness. Across from where the ill man lay, a priest was cremating a dead body on a funeral pyre. Here Siddhartha learned about death.

Siddhartha became extremely dissatisfied with his life after learning about the transience of all things. "What happiness can there be found in life when everything shall be taken from us at death?" Siddhartha wondered. Upon this reflection of death, Siddhartha's dissatisfaction soon became intolerable. He needed to find a way out. He needed to find a way out of dissatisfaction, a way out of the eminent death which follows life. He knew that to succeed in his quest, he must begin by finding a way out of the care of his father, his wife, and the comforts of the palace.

It was not easy for Siddhartha to leave the universe of comfort that he knew. His father's will was an invisible weight that held him down, bound to the luxuries of the palace. One of Siddhartha's greatest obstacles to freeing himself from the palace was his attachment to engaging in the sexual comforts he experienced with his wife and the many beautiful courtesans his father retained in the palace. Just as Siddhartha intended to leave, he would be persuaded into sexual comfort and would be waylaid from beginning his journey.

One morning Siddhartha woke up very early. He saw his court in a strange fog and a dark hue of dawn. Siddhartha looked in shock at the sleeping courtesans. These women, who had always seemed so beautiful and enchanting now looked grotesque and somehow ridiculous as they slept. Instead of being enthralled by their beauty he was repelled by their ugliness.

Seeing his desire for sensual comfort lift, Siddhartha knew that now was his only chance to leave the palace. With the assistance of his best friend and servant, Siddhartha quickly packed his mount and departed.

Far from the palace, in the Southern jungles of the kingdom, Siddhartha and his friend came across a small group of wandering ascetics. Siddhartha asked his friend who the men were. His friend told him that they were men who seek freedom from the world through meditation. Siddhartha wanted this freedom, and so joined the ascetics. Siddhartha's friend didn't understand why he sought freedom and asked him to return with him to the palace. Siddhartha would not and asked his friend to stay with him and find freedom. But Siddhartha's friend only wanted the comforts of the palace. Accordingly the two friends left each other on separate paths.

Siddhartha studied with the ascetics for six years. In that time he mastered all of their disciplines. His practice was to destroy all desires and attachments by engaging in severe mental and physical disciplines. Siddhartha would concentrate for long periods of time ignoring hunger, pain, cold, and heat. Yet after six years of struggle on a path that was supposed to make him free, his dissatisfaction only grew worse!

One day, sitting exhausted under a tree at the side of a river, he finally realized that although he had gained mastery in concentration and focus, in awareness of subtle-physical structures, nonattachment to the physical body, and the use of internal power, that his heart still ached and he was still not free.

As Siddhartha pondered his dissatisfaction of accomplishing so much and yet becoming even more unhappy, a small boat traversing the river passed before him. On the boat, a music teacher was instructing his student. The student played a stringed instrument producing a very flat and dull sound. The teacher said, "It cannot be too loose." The student adjusted the instrument and played again producing a very sharp and tense sound. The teacher said, "But, it cannot be too tight." The student adjusted the instrument and played again, this time producing a sound musically whole, full, magical and bright!

This was Siddhartha's second spiritual lesson from music, and from this lesson he instantly realized the pathway to Enlightenment, what he called "the Middle Way." The Middle Way is neither the path of indulgence on the one hand nor the path of severe discipline on the other. It is the path between the two extremes. In later years, one of Buddha's primary teachings was to ask his students, "When you tune a lute, do you tighten the strings too tight? Or do you leave them too loose? No, you tune them just in the middle! In this way, you must lead a wise life, neither too loose nor too tight, and then you can come to the liberation of the middle path."

After realizing the Middle Way, he stood up from where he had fasted and meditated for so long. He went to the river, where a young woman offered him food. He accepted the food and offered it to the other ascetic Yogis in his order. They were shocked and angered by Siddhartha's negligence of discipline and vows. Siddhartha shared his realization of the Middle Way, but his peers rejected his insight and rejected him from their order.

Siddhartha went out on his own, walking the middle path. He sat under a tree, known as the Bodhi Tree, and resolved to awaken and be free. While in meditation, he was confronted by Mara, the forces of fear, doubt, and confusion that come to all who sit in meditation seeking Enlightenment. Siddhartha faced Mara with wisdom. He touched all the thoughts and energies of fear and confusion, all the threats and temptations of Mara with harmlessness and detachment. All thoughts and energies, all worlds and dimensions, all angels and demons were illuminated and perfect in Siddhartha's mind.

Just as the sun began to rise, he exclaimed, "Freed am I at last!" He had awakened to Nirvana, eternal awareness and peace beyond all of the changing conditions of the world. He was now known as the Buddha, the Awakened One.

Learning from the Buddha Now

Free from suffering and awakened to eternity, the Buddha saw others still trapped in suffering. He saw that all beings want to be happy, but don't know the way to true happiness. In confusion they do things that lead them to continued suffering.

Moved by compassion, Buddha stood from his seat under the Bodhi Tree and began to teach the way to eternal happiness, the pathway to Enlightenment. He traveled across India for 45 years teaching the Dharma, the way to truth and liberation.

Buddha's teachings spread throughout Asia. New forms and elucidations of Buddha's teachings came into being by Enlightened masters who had awoken to the Buddha way. Zen Buddhism, the Bodhisattva way, Tantra, and other forms of Buddhism have re-codified the truths Buddha taught, reaching and inspiring new lands, cultures, and generations. Each new destination adapts the essence of Buddha's teachings to the time, conditions, and the environment for relevant application.

The essence of Buddhist teachings can work for you now, right here in the West. It's not living in a monastery that brings you truth. It's not immersing yourself in another culture that brings you truth. It's not shaving your head and wearing a robe that brings you truth. What brings you truth is the awareness of life itself.

That's the great thing about the truth. The truth is true here and now, just as your life is here and now! Buddha taught eternal truths that were true for him 2500 years ago in India, true for Bodhidharma over 1000 years later when he founded Zen, and true for you today.

So we shall examine the truth of life and the teachings Buddha taught to become Enlightened. This will not be a cerebral exercise in cognitively understanding truth. Our examination will show you that the truth Buddha taught applies directly to you, your life, and your situation, now!

What Is Buddhism?

Buddhism is a way of life. Though religious forms of Buddhism exist today, originally Buddhism was not a religion. Religions focus on an external awareness of truth. Buddhism focuses on an internal awareness of truth.

There is a story that illustrates the difference between the outer and inner focus on truth. A Christian priest and a Buddhist monk were sitting alone in a field. All of a sudden, Jesus appeared! Jesus said, "This is the way to god!" He pointed up into the sky and then disappeared.

The Christian priest immediately wrote the event down. He described what Jesus looked like and how he stood. He described how Jesus pointed and what he said. He interpreted existing *Bible* passages to ascertain the meaning of Jesus' appearance at this time. He noted his conclusions and made plans for incorporating them into the church library. He determined rules of conduct and observances for his congregation based on this event.

The Buddhist monk on the other hand immediately looked up into the sky to learn what Jesus was pointing to.

The Buddha simply pointed a way to Enlightenment just as Jesus pointed a way to god. Religion will teach you how to stand and point; Buddhism will teach you to look and see.

Religions have rules. Buddhism has no rules. Religions teach what is good and what is sin. Buddhism teaches that there is no good and that there is no sin, just different levels of truth. Religion can be known conceptually. Buddhism can only be known by awareness through experience.

To know a city, one person is content by looking at maps and reading articles about the city. Another person spends time shopping, dining, and going to the museums and theaters around town to know a city. Who really knows the city? It doesn't matter! What matters is how much you enjoy your experience. People who are drawn to Buddhism enjoy the freedom of seeking truth in their own experience of life.

Buddhism is a structured methodology expertly designed to bring individuals step-by-step from suffering, fear, and the darkness of the heart to unbound peace, eternal happiness, and the Enlightenment of the spirit. Buddhism exposes eternal truths of life. With truth as the foundation, Buddhism instructs us in how to be happy and free.

Buddhism is helpful in the short-term. In the short-term, it brings you a light of truth in a dark world. Each encounter with Buddhism, each lesson taken to heart, each realization and open-minded intention for the truth, brings you into a brighter and happier condition of life.

Therefore, Buddhism brings a powerful and beautiful promise to all of us! The promise is that no matter how messed up things are in your life and the world, you can always follow the steps of Buddhist teachings out of darkness and into a greater condition of truth and peace. No matter how bad things are, Buddhism leads you into a brighter, happier, and more balanced state of mind and reality.

Buddhism is also helpful in the long-term. In the long-term, it brings you to the direct awareness of the nature of life, beyond suffering, to the ecstatic unity of all things: Nirvana. So in the end, you get ultimate liberation, god-realization, Enlightenment, and cosmic consciousness! All this at no extra cost.

So Buddhism is a way to Enlightenment. It is a way designed by the Buddha, who had himself successfully attained Enlightenment. Just as you can learn how to make a lot of money in real estate from a real estate tycoon, you can learn how to be liberated from an Enlightened person. Just as you can follow a structured educational system and learn to be a doctor from doctors in a university, you can follow a spiritual educational system and learn Enlightenment from an Enlightened person in a spiritual school. Someone who has mastered a discipline or endeavor can provide you with the secrets to success in that field.

On one occasion, while the Buddha was traveling down the road in India, he was approached by a curious man. The man, seeing this luminous exalted being, asked, "Excuse me, are you a god?"

The Buddha answered, "No."

The man questioned again, "Then are you an angel or celestial spirit?"

Again the Buddha answered, "No."

"Then, are you a man?" the man wondered.

The Buddha answered, "No."

The man, now quite perplexed, questioned, "Then what are you?"

The Buddha looked him directly in the eyes and said, "I am awake."

At this the man glimpsed the shining nature of reality. In his realization of truth, a tear ran down his cheek and he said, "Thank you. Thank you for showing me the way to life." Then the man bowed to the Buddha and walked on.

Buddha is not someone to deify, worship, pray to, or get things from. Rather, Buddha is someone to admire and learn from.

Buddha taught his students to be skeptical of all stories, philosophies, dogmas, and teachings. Buddha told the students not to merely believe him and take his teachings on faith. He told them to try them out. That way, they would know from experience whether his teachings were true. Therefore our own experience is the primary teacher in Buddhism.

Just as if you read books about dance and regularly attend the ballet, you won't experience the powerful awareness of dancing unless you yourself dance.

If you hear artists speak of pottery and see them craft ornate vases, you won't know that wonder of creation unless you sit at the wheel and ignite the kiln.

It is also this way in spirituality and Enlightenment. Reading books about Enlightenment gives you a type of information. Hearing lectures from Buddhist monks and yogis gives you a type of information. However, in spirituality, the essential information is provided by yourself and gained through attention to your own experience. In the experience of life, we come to know the power, awareness, and wonder of life.

In Buddhism, there is no need for faith or belief in stories. There is instead an active awareness of truth in the experience of this moment of your own life.

What is important is not what you believe, but what truth you are aware of. Buddhism seeks the facts of reality. Buddhism teaches you to learn for yourself the reality of reality. In Buddhism, we use the perception of our own experience and let go of all concepts and even hopes. Buddhists follow the old saying, "The fool discards what he sees for what he thinks. The wise discards what he thinks for what he sees."

Following the Buddha's prescription for awareness, observe the experience of your own life. See what evolves you and engage in that. See what does not evolve you and disengage from that.

Buddhist Stories

Buddhism has stories too. Buddhist stories never profess to be the complete truth; rather, like any good story, they are models that point you to your own awareness of the truth. Buddhist stories expose balanced understandings of life and eternal views of the spirit. Revealing the most noble qualities of your own mind, Buddhist stories draw you into a greater awareness of life.

There was once a lay practitioner of Zen named Taro. Taro worked in his family's carpentry business, yet he was also a committed student of Zen and would read the spiritual sutras and practice meditation every evening.

On Saturdays, Taro would go to a nearby Zen temple to receive instruction from the monks. He had been preparing for several years to receive a special Koan instruction from the Enlightened Zen master of the temple. Taro had learned that Koans were illogical questions or statements like, "What is the sound of one hand clapping?" or "The nose causes the tail."

After receiving the Koan, a student would need to meditate deeply to find the answer. Finding the answer would bring the student to a powerful spiritual transformation. Koan instruction was rarely given to lay practitioners and would offer Taro a rare opportunity to meet the inaccessible Zen master. Taro was looking forward to this upcoming teaching, yet dutifully spent his days working in the family shop with his two younger brothers.

Taro's youngest brother was very rowdy, boisterous, and quick to anger. His other brother was very sad and gloomy, always slouching his shoulders and wearing a frown.

One day, his unruly youngest brother came into the shop late for work.

"Where have you been?" Taro asked his tardy brother.

"I was listening to the old man's stories," his brother blurted out.

For some years, an old beggar would sit out on the street corner early in the mornings and tell stories for an offering of rice in his bowl. Mostly children would listen on their way to school.

"Aren't you a little old for children's stories?" Taro asked his brother.

"I saw that the children didn't have any rice for the beggar today!" his brother retorted. "And they were good stories!"

"You gave him your breakfast!" Taro exclaimed.

"So what?" his younger brother yelled.

Now the middle brother walked over and said in his usual mope, "We have so much work to do today, I don't think we'll be able to take a lunch break."

"Fine!" the youngest brother yelled as Taro shook his head in disapproval. The three brothers worked the whole day in an unsettled silence.

For the next few weeks the youngest brother came to work late. Each morning he would take his rice and give it to the old beggar as an offering and listen to his stories. Each day he came to the shop late Taro would shake his head in disapproval. In the beginning this would incite an argument and a long day of working in a cold silence.

After a couple of weeks, the youngest brother stopped getting upset when Taro would shake his head and admonish him. A couple of weeks later, the elder brothers came to realize that their youngest brother had changed. He was no longer loud and quick to anger; he was pleasant, forgiving, and kind.

Taro was perplexed by his youngest brother's transformation, but kept on shaking his head in disapproval every day the youngest brother would come into work late. To his great dismay a few days later, the middle brother was gone from breakfast and showed up to work late. Both of his brothers were offering their breakfast and listening to the stories of the old beggar.

Taro was very upset in the beginning and would shake his head in disappointment every morning when his younger brothers came into work late. After a couple of weeks Taro's anger fell away as he started to see that the middle brother was no longer frowning and gloomy all the time. A couple of weeks later, the middle brother started smiling regularly and carried on in joyful conversations with the youngest brother.

Soon the time came for Taro to receive his Koan instruction. As he set out to the temple to receive his teaching, he saw his brothers sitting with the children and listening to the beggar. With plenty of time to spare and growing curiosity, Taro decided to see what kind of stories the old beggar told to ascertain why his brothers seemed to like them so much.

Taro, fetching his lunch from his bag, joined his brothers and the children out on the corner of the street. Taro gave his lunch as alms to the beggar and the old beggar began to tell a story.

The old beggar told a story of a frog that was happy jumping amongst the lily pads and was never unhappy like other frogs because he didn't hunt flies.

Taro was somehow transported to a beautiful luminous place in his mind as he listened to the story. After the story, the teller and the listeners all sat in a peaceful silence, smiling. In time the old beggar thanked the listeners for the rice and went on his way.

Taro donned his robes and continued on his way to the Zen temple to receive his special Koan instruction. When arriving to the temple, he was ushered into the Zen master's quarters for the special instruction. He knelt before the famous Zen master and bowed.

After a moment of silence the Zen master began the Koan. He started, "There once was a happy frog." As the Zen master spoke the next words, Taro quickly recognized that the Koan was identical to the story that the old beggar had told him earlier in the morning.

Perplexed he looked to the Zen master with a questioning expression. The Zen master smiled as he continued with the Koan. Just then, Taro realized that the famous Zen master in Buddhist priest robes sitting before him was in fact the same beggar who had been telling stories on the street corner for years!

In the wonder of profound spiritual realization, Taro said, "The children's stories are all Koans!"

The Zen master nodded and concluded the teaching.

Stories are an integral aspect of Buddhist study. Just as Buddha himself used stories, many spiritual teachers use stories to teach the truths of Enlightenment. Buddhist stories are stories of life that point to powerful inner truths. When you learn the stories, you learn ways of connecting to bright dimensions of understanding that exist within you!

Once, a young man who had just become a Buddhist monk lay down to sleep for the first time in his new bed in the monastery. He shared a very large bedroom with over a dozen other monks.

When the lights were out and everyone was tucked in, one of the monks in the far corner of the room yelled out, "9!" A moment later, all the monks giggled.

A minute later another monk next to him yelled out, "101!" A moment later, all the monks laughed loudly. Then someone yelled, "48!" All of the monks roared with laughter.

The new monk was quite perplexed by now, but he decided to yell out a number as a gesture to fit in with everyone. He yelled out, "26!" A moment later, all the monks groaned with displeasure. After that everyone went to sleep.

The next morning as the monks washed before meditation practice, the new monk asked one of the older monks, "Why do people laugh when someone calls out a number at night before we go to sleep?"

The older monk answered, "For years we've told the same jokes together before going to bed. Our Zen jokes tend to take a very long time before you get to the punch-line. After a while we just memorized the jokes and gave them each a number. So this way it is easier and faster for us to tell and get to the laughs!"

"Oh I see!" the new monk said with a smile. "But then why did everyone groan when I called out the number 26?"

Shaking his head, the older monk said, "That is just a really bad joke!"

So in Buddhism, you gotta know your numbers! Buddhist stories don't only tell of truth; they also give you reference numbers to the truth in your life. Buddhist stories are referenceable by many of life's experiences. When you know the stories, you gain deeper insight into the experiences of your life.

The Story of the Wheel of Life

One of Buddhism's stories explains how life works for all beings. This cosmology story is called the Wheel of Life.

Buddhist cosmology is simple. There's no ultimate heaven or hell. That's silly! Rather, there are ten thousand heavens and ten thousand hells. In Buddhism there is not just one ultimate god, or one pantheon of gods. Rather, there are ten thousand ultimate gods and ten thousand pantheons of gods. Buddhism tells that there are countless worlds with countless beings.

Buddhists see life for all beings in all worlds as a wheel—a wheel of birth, growth, adolescence, maturation, aging, sickness, decay, and death. Death leads directly to new life. In Buddhism, it's not a straight shot from birth to death, and then some eternal afterlife. Life is an endless causal cycle. So in Buddhism, there's really no beginning and no ending; there really isn't even a middle. Who's to say where the circle starts, where it ends, or where its middle is?

All beings exist in this causal wheel of life. There are however, different layers of the wheel. There are magnificent gods in the high heavens, lesser gods in paradise realms, humans and animals here on Earth, ghosts in the shadow realms, and suffering masses in the hells. Depending on the goodness of one's merit, beings may ascend or descend within the wheel of life. The final truth of the wheel of life is that anywhere within the wheel there is great transience and suffering.

Humans are toward the top of the middle layers. Our layer, or realm of being, is characterized by a dynamic range of physical and mental suffering. Humans can also experience periods of great joys. The human realm of being is considered to be very auspicious in Buddhism because it is a level where the suffering, desire, and unawareness of the hell, ghost, and animal realms does not completely obstruct one from seeking Enlightenment. As well, the magical, wondrous, and divine realms of the demigods and gods don't hold one in so much transient comfort so that one becomes attached to these comforts and sees no reason to seek Enlightenment.

In the realms of being above us exist lesser gods and higher gods. Lesser gods, though powerful and holy, suffer greatly in conflicts of power amongst their peers, jealousy of the higher gods, and great fear of losing their power and dominion.

Higher gods have wondrous vast lifetimes in paradise heavens. Yet they suffer tremendously at the time of their death. The wheel of life story tells that gods are born and die, just as universes are created and destroyed in the timelessness of Nirvana.

Just below the human realm of being in the wheel of life are animals. Animals are deeply locked into the experience and effects of their biological function. Animals suffer greatly from fear and primal desires. They lack the ability to apprehend greater opportunities of awareness.

Below the level of animals are disembodied beings, also called hungry ghosts due to their extreme suffering from desire. Below these unhappy spirits of the shadows are the lowest regions of the wheel of life, the hells. Beings incarnated in hell suffer greatly from physical torment, fear, and horrific visions.

Though the wheel of life that Buddha described referred to different types of beings and the different worlds that they take form in, the deeper truth in his teaching is that the wheel of life primarily exists in your mind. We all experience times where we act like animals, acting and reacting in the relegation of our biology and the body consciousness. And at other times we can desire money, material possessions, relationships, and position to the point of despair equal to the beings in the realms of the hungry ghosts. Also as human beings we can experience times in which we achieve great victories, are in admired positions in which we have a strong influence over others, or reach extraordinary peaks in our awareness of life and of ourselves. At these times we feel as high, powerful, and vast as gods. Also as human beings we can experience times in which we feel tremendous anger, depression, fear, and darkness. At these times we are so unhappy and dark in our hearts that we feel as though we are in hell.

The wheel of life spins in your mind. Heaven and hell is primarily experienced in your mind. Though there are hells as real as this Earth, hell is most commonly reached with dark-minded anger, depression, and evil intentions. Though there are heavens as real as this Earth, heaven is most commonly reached with love, forgiveness, humility, and compassion.

Once there was a renowned samurai who petitioned a famous Zen master for spiritual guidance. Kneeling, the samurai set his helmet aside, bowed, and politely asked the Zen master, "Please master, teach me about heaven and hell. I have killed many men in my lifetime and fear that I will go to hell when finally I die. Can you show me the way to heaven? I will devote myself to your teachings and do whatever is necessary to find heaven and escape hell."

The Zen master made a sour frown. He shook his head in denial saying, "A clumsy oaf-butcher like you could never understand even if I told you. You are far too ignorant and unaware." Pointing toward the door, the Zen master shouted, "Get your uncouth barbarian face out of my sight!"

At this tremendous insult, the samurai became infuriated. He had never been spoken to with such rudeness and was now livid. "How dare you speak to me like that?" the samurai roared. The Zen master sat unresponsively motionless, still pointing toward the door.

Incited further by the Zen master's stubborn defiance, the samurai's anger exploded into a fiery rage. He leaped to his feet and pulled his sword from its sheath saying, "I will kill you for your insult!"

As the samurai furiously raised his sword high above his head, the Zen master, calmly drew his pointing finger to point directly toward the samurai's face and said, "This is hell."

Just before his final movement of releasing the sword's swing into the deathblow, the samurai paused. In that moment the samurai realized that the Zen master was showing him the blunder of his ways, the very thing he feared that would bring him to hell. The samurai immediately felt humbled. He sheathed his sword and fell to his knees. "Forgive me master," the samurai said. "I now understand how I bring myself my own hell." The samurai tossed his sheathed sword to the side and bowed kneeling with his forehead on the ground before the Zen master saying, "You have shown me the errors of my ways. I am forever grateful."

The Zen master now pointed to the samurai as he bowed before him and remarked, "And this is heaven."

Even though hell seems pretty bad, and heaven seems pretty good, they both ultimately have one thing in common: suffering. All beings in hell, heaven, or here on Earth are unfulfilled, dissatisfied and in spiritual suffering.

As Buddha taught of the wheel of life, he pointed out that the Enlightened exist outside of the wheel. He said that in Enlightenment you escape the suffering of the wheel of life. So the point of Buddhism is not to get you from

Earth to heaven, but beyond the transient births and deaths that cause so much suffering. The point of Buddhism is to free you from the wheel of life altogether. Buddha said that he had defeated death. He taught that the realization of Enlightenment was an awakening unto immortality beyond the causal cycle of existence, an awakening unto the bliss of eternity beyond the wheel of life.

The Story of Reincarnation

Your spirit is eternal! It learns, grows, and develops in each lifetime through experiences in life and spiritual practice. Your spirit never dies. Unlike your physical body, which becomes sick, grows old, and eventually dies, your soul lives on forever. We are all spirits on this eternal journey.

In each lifetime, your spirit comes into a physical body at birth and has experiences in the world. At the end of your life, your physical body is left behind, and the spirit's journey continues into a new life with a new physical body. Your state of mind at death determines the condition of your next life. This process of birth, death, and rebirth, called reincarnation, is a fundamental Buddhist understanding.

Each one of us determines what to do with our lives. It's up to you! As practicing Buddhists, we use our lives and experiences as vehicles to advance our spirit. Through meditation, mindfulness, and other Buddhist practices, you can experience greater truth and Enlighten your spirit.

Understanding reincarnation helps us in two ways. First, we realize that we can enjoy life and not fear death. We know that we have endless opportunities to change, grow, and experience life. Death doesn't scare us, because we understand that our spirit will not die and we will live again.

Second, the understanding of reincarnation helps us to prepare for our next life. The spiritual knowledge we gain in each lifetime is retained by our eternal soul, so it is never lost. We can consciously decide to advance on the pathway to Enlightenment so that we will be happier in this life and in our next life.

The Buddha said, "Who shall conquer this world and the world of death with all its gods? You shall, even as the man who seeks flowers finds the most beautiful, the rarest."

The Story of Karma

Karma literally means "action." It is the law of cause and effect. Your karma now is the result of everything you've ever done. Not only is it everything you've ever done in this lifetime, but it is also everything you've ever done in all of your past lives! All of the actions, inactions, and experiences that you ever had have led you precisely to your current state of mind, awareness, and the seat you're sitting in now.

Padmasambhava, an Enlightened teacher in Tibet said, "If you want to know your past life, look into your present condition. If you want to know your future life, look at your present actions."

Karma is initiated by the intent behind your actions. Regardless of the magnitude of an act, its karmic quality is determined solely by the purity of intent of the person performing the act.

Thoughts are the primary actions that concern Buddhists. Thinking impure thoughts is the cause for negative and obscured awareness. Negative and obscured awareness is the cause of suffering and negative physical manifestations. Thinking angry thoughts about someone is as harmful to your peace of mind as physically assaulting them.

The cycle of negative and positive karmas that we create for ourselves binds us to the wheel of life, the endless cycle of birth, death, and rebirth. Karma is the primary force behind reincarnation. Our karmas cause us to be reborn again, to experience the results of our previous actions. The karmic condition of our next birth is determined solely by our state of mind at the time of our death.

Many people inaccurately view karma as fate. They throw their hands up in the air and say, "I'll get the job if I'm meant to be happy working as a computer programmer and I won't get it if I'm meant to be miserable slaving away at Burger King."

This view is incorrect because it implies that we have no control over our current situation in this life or in our future lives. The truth is that we do have control over our karma because of our free will.

Free will is the good news because it allows us to change ourselves and improve our minds at any time! We can decide to change our future by deciding to change our karma now.

The Tibetan Book of Living and Dying tells us, "Karma means our ability to create and to change. It is creative because we can determine how and why we act. We can change."

Karma is under our control! Through our command of free will we can choose to be happy. We can choose to take classes to become a computer programmer instead of a Burger King employee. We can choose to follow Buddhist teachings to Enlightenment instead of feeling miserable. We can radically change our destiny in every moment. There is no fate but what we make.

Free will is the ability to change the karma that was about to become your future. Free will is the beginning of the end of the cycle of karma and reincarnation. With our free will we can follow Buddhist teachings to Enlightenment and erase self-identification from all actions. When there is no self associated with action, then action is pure, perfect, and harmless. When Enlightened, our actions become the movement of life with no one causing them and no one there to experience the effects of them. Enlightenment is the only way to be liberated from the binding chains of karma.

The Adventure Begins!

Buddhism is a journey. It is a journey of self-discovery. It is a journey into now. It is a journey from ignorance to wisdom, from suffering to bliss, and from darkness into light.

So the adventure begins! Actually it's already begun. Buddhist teachings lead you on a fantastic and most excellent adventure! Buddhist teachings bring you on a journey into the complete awareness of your life.

The spiritual path is the greatest adventure in the universe! All other endeavors yield only temporary rewards and transient satisfactions. The journey to Enlightenment is the only endeavor that yields infinite reward and eternal satisfaction.

If you climbed the highest mountain, you could find some happiness and fulfillment, but in time it wouldn't be enough. If you raised a good family, built a fine house, and became a model citizen, you could find some happiness and fulfillment, but in time it wouldn't be enough. If you built a billion dollar business, became #1 over Tiger Woods in golf, and went on to be a famous movie star and rock star, you could find some happiness and fulfillment, but in time it still wouldn't be enough. You would not find eternal satisfaction or ultimate fulfillment in these endeavors.

The adventure of Enlightenment is very different from other endeavors because it is quite the opposite of other endeavors. All other undertakings are carried out for self-gaining. We want to gain experiences, possessions, love, and well, everything for the fulfillment of the self. The pathway to Enlightenment is undertaken to surrender the self that seeks to gain fulfillment.

It sounds paradoxical but when you let go of the limited self that seeks fulfillment, you discover the unlimited self that is completely fulfilled. The unlimited self sees that everything you've ever wanted is already within you, that you are complete with nothing lacking.

As you move ahead on your adventure, it's helpful to study Buddha's central teachings of Enlightenment. Reflecting on these essential lessons of truth and liberation will aid you greatly on your quest. Learning these key lessons will give you a solid understanding of the foundation of the pathway to Enlightenment.

The Four Noble Truths are the foundation of Buddhist teachings. These are truths for all beings. These are truths about life—your life. These are truths that lead to freedom—your freedom.

The First Noble Truth is that there is suffering and pain in life. The Second Noble Truth is that there is a primary cause to suffering. The Third Noble Truth is that there is an end to suffering. The Fourth Noble Truth is that the teachings of Enlightenment, what Buddha called the Eightfold Path, are the way out of suffering.

Now we will review the Four Noble Truths in a little more detail. This way you can see how these truths that Buddha spoke of 2,500 years ago are important factors of liberation in your life today.

The First Noble Truth

The First Noble Truth is the truth of suffering. We all experience suffering. We want true, everlasting happiness and well-being, but the happiness and joy that we experience never lasts. Our transient joys in life inevitably turn into sorrows. We can better our situation in life, but even if we raised ourselves to heaven, we would still ultimately greatly suffer.

Why is this? It is because for all beings on the wheel of life, there is a clinging to a sense of a separate self. All animals, humans, and gods see the universe in terms of self and other.

In this grand illusion of separateness, we lose awareness of the essential truth of life: unity. Lacking the complete awareness of unity, all beings suffer from the limited awareness of partiality. Enlightenment is the absence of a separate self. Enlightenment is the intimate awareness of unity.

Suffering is not hierarchical. A homeless child dying of hunger in a third world country may suffer much less than a high school debutante whose daddy refuses to buy her a pair of new Gucci shoes to match her new Lexus graduation present. The amount you suffer depends on your spiritual awareness of unity.

This is why the Buddha said that even the gods praise the one who is awakened and Enlightened to the unity of all things. Enlightened beings don't suffer because they are in union with all things in the eternality of the universe.

All things are a perfection of unity. Quantum physics has even scientifically proven this ancient Buddhist truth, yet our awareness remains in separateness despite the truth.

Unaware of unity, the beginning of our every thought, feeling, concept, and idea comes from our separateness from the universe and not from our union with all things in the universe. At the foundation of our spirit, this movement of separateness unbalances everything else in our lives.

We are as trees without roots, reaching with our branches and leaves to the sky and the sun, but lying fallen over at our base. We are building the palace of our lives on an unstable foundation. Although we build a beautiful and expansive castle, all eventually crumbles.

Before the time of the Buddha, Enlightened teachers of the mystery schools of Egypt knew this truth well, and they taught their students the foundation of unity through the study of architecture and the masonry work of building pyramids.

The point of a pyramid is the point of the pyramid, pardon the pun. The top stone itself is the shape of the whole. The top stone resides high in the heavens in union with the sky. Yet the top stone could not be in union with the heavens unless it was in union with its foundation.

There are two primary types of suffering that beings experience. The first is the suffering of pain. The second is the suffering of change.

The Suffering of Pain

The first type of suffering is physical and mental pain. Life is pain. This is the first teaching for Buddhist monks and a fundamentally important one. If you can read or hear these words, you will experience pain at some time.

Even though we know there is a certain amount of pain in life, we don't like pain right off the bat. Pain plain hurts, so we try to do what we can to steer clear of pain. Because we see pain as so completely bad, we develop strong aversion to pain, and that aversion actually causes us to experience more pain.

We feel vulnerable and vigorously over-defend against anything that could cause us pain. It's as if we were so concerned for our tender soles as we walk down the path that we veer from the sharp pebbles before us and find ourselves accidentally walking into mounds of broken glass on the side of the road. Instead, we should learn from the Buddha that though there may be some sharp pebbles, the middle of the path is the right way.

There was once a student who complained to his Buddhist teacher that life was too painful and that he couldn't practice because he had too much pain.

The teacher walked the student over to an expansive lake. The teacher fetched water from the lake into a tea cup. The teacher then reached into a bag of salt and poured a handful of salt into the tea cup.

"Here," the teacher said to the student, "Drink this."

The student, a bit puzzled, drank the water from the tea cup. As soon as he had taken a sip of the water, he immediately spit it out, scowled, and said, "Yuck! That tastes awful!"

His teacher said, "There is a certain amount of pain in life. When your mind is so small and limited, the pain is unbearable." The teacher then reached into the bag of salt and poured a handful of salt into the lake. "Now drink from the lake," the teacher ordered.

The student knelt down and drank from the lake. "Refreshing!" he remarked with a satisfied smile.

"When your mind is as vast as the great lake, the pain in life is bearable."

It is so important to have a proper and realistic outlook on life. You can't expect life to be painless. Life doesn't turn out as it does on TV sitcoms. Many people have very unrealistic ideas of how life should be. So this is why the first lesson in Buddhism is that life is pain. As my teacher used to say, "If anyone tells you different, they're either lying to you or trying to sell you something."

Human life is characterized by suffering and ignorance. It's as if you've accidentally stepped into a bear trap. You know those traps with two large iron jaws and jagged teeth that close on the unsuspecting animal which steps on its pressure point trigger? Well, it's as if you have triggered just such a trap and the iron jaws are clamped shut on your leg.

Your leg is hurting, bleeding, and beginning to fester. Your efforts to extricate yourself from the painful iron jaws just seem to cause you more bleeding and pain. Unaware of how to help yourself, you walk along, limping with your constant companion.

Finally, you come to someone who says that they know how to get out of the painful trap, because they once were stuck in a similar trap and learned the secret of liberation.

You start focusing on your suffering to apply the secrets of liberation, but find that you get caught up in the story of your suffering just as you begin.

Upon reflection of your suffering, you want to know who set the trap, what their intent was, and if you can sue them. You also want to know what kind of bear the trap is for, why three of the trap's teeth are longer than the others, and why it hurts you more in the back than the front.

So when facing their suffering, people tend to be more interested in the story of their suffering than in attending to the things they have to do to extricate themselves from their suffering.

Human life is characterized by suffering and fear. It's as if we suffer from hunger. We sit in a dark room, where we can only see crusts of bread on the floor near us for sustenance. The room is so dark and cold that we're afraid to explore, to move beyond the area we know, because there may be no bread crusts there. Unwilling to take a chance, fearing our starvation, we sit in our little dark area, barely surviving as we scramble around looking for the meager crusts of bread.

Little do we know that the cold, dark room we are in has a light switch, a heater, and a grand table of food. There is a cornucopia of cheeses and meats, bread and fruit, vegetables and grains. In the same room where we cling to crusts of bread, there is an all-sustaining feast. Out of our fear and ignorance, we stay in the dark without seeking a light and remain unaware that everything we need for life is right before us.

We think that the scarcity of crusts of bread makes us suffer. We think that the darkness and the coldness of the room make us suffer. However, it is not the conditions and events of life that cause our suffering. It is fear, ignorance, and lack of awareness of the perfection of reality that cause our suffering.

My Buddhist teacher was a mystical healer. He was able to cure serious illnesses such as cancer, illness-causing habits such as smoking and overeating, as well as mental illnesses such as depression. He healed many people, mostly his students and their families, but would heal anyone that a student would bring to him for help.

On one occasion an older monk in my spiritual school was diagnosed with an inoperable brain tumor. His prognosis was death in less than eight months.

His younger brother, a businessman, went to console him. His consolation efforts seemed unnecessary. His brother, the ill monk, seemed rather happy. The younger brother wondered why. The ill monk told him that he asked his Buddhist master for healing, and if it were the Dharma for him to be well, he would soon be well.

His brother, knowing the diagnosis, worried that his older brother was simply in denial. However, staying close to his older brother for the next few months, seeing the MRI scans every couple weeks, as well as the shock and amazement of the doctors as the inoperable brain tumor shrank and disappeared from his brother's head, he was filled with wonder and asked if he could have a meeting with the mystical healing Buddhist master. His now completely healthy older brother arranged a meeting for him.

When he met my Buddhist teacher, my teacher asked, "What can I help you with?"

The man said, "Last week, I dropped a 21-inch TV on my left foot. See look, you can still see the bruise. And now that I'm getting older, my lower back starts to hurt when I sit on the couch too long. Also, I get a sharp pain in my shoulder during my golf swing on the long drives. And when I talk a lot like this, my jaw starts popping a little." He pointed to the right side of his cheek, opened and closed his mouth, and said, "See what I mean?"

My teacher nodded and said, "Oh yes, I see."

The man went on, "In the past few months, I've put on a few pounds. My wife nags me to exercise more. I really get frustrated, because my favorite cardigan doesn't fit very well anymore. And my wife is Italian and makes a rich, spicy meatball dish every Thursday night. I love the meatballs, but I always get a terrible case of heartburn after eating them." The man then counted on his fingers to make sure he didn't miss anything and then said, "All of this is so painful. Can you heal me?"

My teacher paused thoughtfully for a moment before saying, "Sorry, I can't help you."

The man looked surprised and said, "But you have the power to heal my brother's cancer; surely you can help me with my pain!"

My teacher went on, "No one can help you with your pain, the way you want help. Not me, not a host of doctors, chiropractors, acupuncturists, massage therapists, god, or the genie of the lamp can help you with your pain. You want dogs not to bite. You want bites not to hurt. You want roses not to have thorns. You want thorns not to prick."

The man looked a bit disenchanted.

After a moment my teacher offered, "I can however help you with the thing that causes you the greatest pain!"

Thrilled, the man said, "Great! So then you'll fix my golf shoulder?"

"No, that's not the thing that causes you the most pain."

The man questioned, "So you'll fix my lower back pain then?"

"No, that's not the thing that causes you the most pain."

"Then what causes my greatest pain?" the man asked.

"The thing that causes your greatest pain," my teacher said, "is that you don't think you should have any pain." The man looked at him curiously. "Everyone experiences pain. Pain is your ally; it reminds you how precious life is. What makes your pain unbearable is the consternation you feel when you don't think you should have any pain."

The man sat motionless for a moment contemplating his condition and my teacher's words. In coming to understand this truth of life, he then smiled, free of his suffering.

D.H. Lawrence wrote in one of his famous poems, "I never saw a wild thing sorry for itself. A small bird will drop frozen dead from a bough without ever having felt sorry for itself." When you get past the idea that life shouldn't be painful and accept the pain of life, the physical pain and mental pressures of life are bearable. What makes physical pain unbearable is the mental pain we affix to it.

Buddhists are sensitive, knowing the truth of suffering for themselves and are compassionate for the suffering of others. However, Buddhists are tough, because they know the truth. Buddhists never indulge in their own pain or cherish their own egos. Buddhists use pain as an ally. Buddhists take the pain and fight for a greater awareness of life.

We've all had painful experiences. Some people close their eyes to life because some of life hurts. Buddhist teachings advise that instead of letting pain shut you down, you should grow from it.

Use pain as an ally. Let pain teach you to be more aware, more controlled and more humble. There are always two ways to go after you get burnt. You are either adverse to the pain and stay away from fire to avoid getting burnt again, or you learn how to use fire properly. The proper use of fire enriches your life and you will not be burnt again.

Assignment: The Truth of Pain

Please open your Enlightenment Journal to a new page. Entitle the page, "The Truth of Pain."

1. First to consider the truth of pain, reflect on the most physical and tangible kind of pain: bodily pain and illness. Recall your own life experiences and write an account of your greatest physical suffering. Write about a time where you were ill or hurt. Describe your physical feelings of the pain or sickness. Did you learn anything from the experience of this pain?

2. Next recall a time where you saw someone else suffer great physical pain or illness. Write an account of what you witnessed in your Enlightenment Journal. Did you learn anything from it, the same way Buddha had learned something about life by witnessing old age and illness?

3. Next reflect on more intangible feelings of pain: mental and emotional pain. From your own life experiences, write an account of your greatest mental or emotional suffering. Write about a time when you felt bad, angry, or depressed. Describe the circumstances and your feelings. Did you learn anything from the experience of this pain?

4. Now recall a time where you saw someone else suffering from mental or emotional pain. Write an account of what you witnessed in your Enlightenment Journal. Did you learn anything from seeing another suffering from this pain?

5. Lastly, in your life, what has been more painful, physical suffering and illness or mental and emotional pain? Write the answer to this question in your Enlightenment Journal.

Complete this assignment now. Continue reading when finished.

The Suffering of Change

The next type of suffering that we experience is the suffering of change. Everything that we can think about or talk about will change. Every person, place, and thing will change. Feelings change, thoughts change, relationships change, people change, understandings change. Everything in our lives is in a constant motion of change.

There is an expansive desert in the Southwest. The dirt where the cactus stands is arid, crumbly, and dry. The formations of mesas and arches are beautiful to behold.

However, what is hot and dry today was once cool and wet. The mesas and the arches were created by an ancient sea that was once there. What is the desert now was once the sea. What is a great mountain today will become a valley in the future. What was a valley in the past is a great mountain today. The Earth and the heavens are constantly changing.

How much more quickly do the notions of humans change? What was fashionable yesterday is comical today. What is seen as politically good today will be seen as politically evil tomorrow. The person who excites and delights you today becomes your greatest sorrow tomorrow. What was something we believed in completely became something we can no longer believe at all. What was right has become wrong. What was wrong has become right.

Life is in constant flux. That's just the way it is. The ancient Chinese text known as the *I Ching*, the book of changes, states that everything in this world that is one way will change into its opposite. What is alive will change to be dead. What is day will change to be night. What is strong will change to be weak.

So, the good news is that everything that you think is bad will change to be good! But be careful, because everything that you think is good will change to be bad! The wisdom of the *I Ching* shows us that instead of being caught up in judging things as good or bad, we should simply observe the sweetness and preciousness of all experience.

The only problem is that we fear change. We cling to a limited sense of self, the ego, which wants nothing to change at all. Why, if anything changes, that would mean we would change. Change means destruction of the reality and self that we've become attached to. This is just not acceptable for an ego! The ego craves certainty in a completely uncertain world.

Once, while it was very hot, a man built a house that had no walls and no roof. He was happy sitting in the sun with the strong breeze from the mountains.

After some days, the sun was not as strong. Some days later, the wind became cold and the sun offered not enough warmth. The man was very upset now. He built a stone stove in his house to keep warm.

As the leaves started to fall from the trees and the winds started to blow colder, with great consternation, the man built walls for his house to keep the winds from chilling him.

As days passed on, it became colder and colder. The man was very upset, huddling next to his stove. As time passed, it became very cold and snow started falling from the sky into his house. The man, quite upset, built a roof for his house. Now he was comfortable for some time.

After a while, he no longer had to burn wood in his stove. Some time later, he started to become warm again. After more days passed, the man became very warm and unsettled in his house. Very upset, he removed his roof and walls to see the shining sun and feel the cool breeze from the hills. Now he was happy again sitting in the sun with the strong breeze.

Soon, the man's old friend came to visit. Seeing that there were no walls and no roof, his friend asked, "What do you intend to do in the winter? The winds will blow cold and snow will fall from the sky!"

The man, shocked and upset, considering the unharmonious possibilities, answered, "Well, I pray to god that will never happen!"

Though the nature of reality is fluid change, the ego is unsettled by change. The ego fights change. The ego tries to control everything. The ego clings to old views and concepts and fights new ones.

The ego tries to fit reality into a changeless model of understanding. Hegel, a prominent 18th century German philosopher, once explained that philosophers build monumental palaces of thought and concept. These palaces of life awe and amaze all who view their spectacle. Unfortunately, unforeseen by the philosopher, life changes the locks on the doors of these fantastic palaces so that no one can live in them, not even the philosopher who created them. Hegel said that the philosopher lives behind the palace in a shack.

Even if we do manage to fit reality into a model, we immediately cut ourselves off from the truth. If life didn't change, it wouldn't be life. Affixing reality into a rigid model obscures the truth of reality.

The ego is like an ice cube that wants to keep its form in a warm glass of water. The ego is like an ocean wave that does not want to crash on the shore. As ridiculous as it seems, some of our greatest suffering comes from just this sort of thing. Our clinging to the past and attempts to control life bring us great sorrows.

Post Assignment

Plastic flowers are very popular these days. Synthetic cloth flowers sometimes even have simulated dew drops on the petals. Plastic flowers and synthetic cloth flowers also last a great deal longer than organic ones.

If you did a ten-year cost analysis, considering the rate of inflation and what you currently spend on flowers, you'd be far better off investing in plastic flowers.

Also, you don't have to change the water and add more flower food for plastic flowers. As well, plastic flowers don't smell bad and drop leaves and petals everywhere when they die. Yep, plastic flowers look perfect, are a far better value, and are much easier to take care of than organic flowers.

So why is it then that you picked a real flower for this assignment? It is because real flowers change! The fact that they change is what makes them so beautiful. The energy of change keeps life precious.

Once a student told his Buddhist teacher about a difficulty he had recently overcome. His teacher remarked, "Change is sweet." A week later, the student came to his teacher to ask advice about a difficulty that had recently arisen for him. His teacher remarked, "Change is sweet."

The fleeting beauty and purity of fresh cut flowers is what we love about them. The purity that you feel in reflecting upon a beautiful flower seems delicate, but in its original aspect that purity is a very powerful force. The flower in full bloom reflects the noon tide of your spirit. The splendor and expression of the flower directs you to the immaculately pure, beautiful, and vibrant dimensions of your own being. So, be open to the sweetness of change and uncertainty. Keep your flower as you will need it in an upcoming assignment.

Change Brings Death

Our greatest fear is that our life will change and become our death. If you have come into existence on this planet, you will go out of existence on this planet. My teacher reminded his students of this fact on many occasions by saying, "There are no survivors on the planet Earth!"

All who are born will die. Death is the final destination of everything that lives. Death is the epitome of our fear of change.

Assignment: What I Know about Death

What do you know about death? What are the stories that you know? What are the ones that you believe?

Entitle a new page in your Enlightenment Journal, "What I Know about Death."

Do you know anyone who has died? Write the story of his or her death.

What are the facts that you know about death? Write an account of everything you know about death as fact.

Complete this assignment now. Continue reading when finished.

Finding Peace in Death

It is difficult for us to find peace and happiness when we are certain of our death. Death seems to be contradictory to peace, happiness, and fulfillment. Why work to safeguard our future and create security for ourselves and our loved ones, if it all has to come to an end?

Eventually everything that brings us peace and happiness will vanish when we die. The security and comfort that we build will be demolished by death. All of our loved ones will be torn from us by death. How can we be happy and find peace while living under a death sentence? Knowing that we will die causes us untold distress and horror.

Chuang Tzu, a famous Taoist master, faced the same quandary. He was hungry one day and wanted to eat something so that he would be sustained, comfortable, and happy. He took his bow and quiver and walked into the forest to hunt. After walking for some time he stopped to look around. He could see no animals.

Looking at the ground, he saw a small insect crawl out from under a leaf in search of food. "How very much alike we are!" he thought to himself. A moment later he saw a praying mantis come out from behind a blade of grass. The mantis was about to attack the small insect when Chuang Tzu noticed a cat springing from behind the bushes to kill the mantis. Just as the cat with its claws drawn neared the mantis, Chuang Tzu noticed a bird of prey launching from a high bough to kill the cat.

"The bird would make a satisfying meal," thought Chuang Tzu. He quickly strung his bow, stepped forward into the clearing, and aimed at the rapidly descending bird. Just then Chuang Tzu realized the eternal truth of life and laughed out loud in his awakening.

Another hunter was not far from Chuang Tzu and mistakenly thought him to be a deer. This hunter had his bow strung and aimed at Chuang Tzu. Just before he let loose his arrow, he heard Chuang Tzu's great laugh and realized he was mistakenly aiming at a man.

The small insect captured its food. The mantis dispatched the small insect. The cat took the life of the mantis. The bird of prey annihilated the cat. The other hunter, seeing the bird, killed it with an arrow. Chuang Tzu laughed again.

The hunter said to Chuang Tzu, "The bird is mine, I shot it first. I thought you were a deer. I almost killed you."

Chuang Tzu answered, "I'm free from death! The bird would have only satisfied me for a short time. My freedom is immortal happiness."

"What do you mean? How can you be free from death?" the hunter asked.

Chuang Tzu answered, "I realized that we all die when we try to fulfill ourselves. We are all caught in a causal chain of death. The only way to transcend the chain of death is to transcend the self altogether! Free of all self-born discord, our spirits ascend into a condition of eternal spiritual happiness beyond death."

Assignment: The Death of a Flower

Observe your flower every day until it dies. Entitle a new page in your Enlightenment Journal, "The Death of a Flower."

Make an Enlightenment Journal entry describing your flower every day until it is dead. Describe the form and energy of your flower. Describe your feelings as you observe it.

When it is dead, throw it away. Don't be attached to its form. Its energy will have passed. Toss it in the trash.

This will be an ongoing assignment that you can do while continuing with the Enlightenment Workbook. Please continue to the next page now.

Death Stories

Death is the primary reason we have religious Big Picture stories. Although the emergence of science has made it difficult for us to buy into religious stories of an afterlife, the scientific outlook holds no spirit, no heart, so we don't feel consoled in not believing in some kind of afterlife.

Is there an afterlife? Is there reincarnation? Or is there just nonexistent oblivion? These questions can be answered by religious stories, scientific stories, and even Buddhist stories. If you believe in them, then you will be taking these stories on faith.

Ultimately, stories just give you intellectual understandings that are separate from truthfully knowing. Belief is what you think, faith is what you hope, and truth is what you know. As much as you want to believe in stories, the partial truth that you gain from them is not real enough to end your suffering of a truth that is very real to you — that you will die.

Even those with complete faith in traditional stories fall short of truth, happiness, and fulfillment when they see evidence that what they believed in is false or that their story does not account for some aspects of their experience.

Take yourself, for example. At one time you, like many people, believed in Santa Claus. You were told that Santa Claus was real and that he had miraculous awareness and powers.

You were told that if you were good, he would reward you. As proof, on Christmas Day you received presents in a spectacular and merry pageant under a decorated tree. You believed this story completely. You understood the rules, risks, and rewards. Your belief made Santa Claus a reality to you, but it was an incomplete and partial reality. The truth ended up being more real.

So how did you stop believing in Santa Claus? Did you find evidence? Did you find all of the toys that you were to receive on Christmas stashed in your parents' closet? Did you see the Santa Claus at the mall drop his beard and hat, revealing a middle-aged plumber? Did you see Mommy kissing Santa Claus underneath the mistletoe?

Or did you see the impossibility of the whole story? Did you, upon seeking and not finding reasonable information to back up the story of flying reindeer and a naughty list, become disenchanted with the whole idea? Did you realize that it was logistically impossible for a single man to deliver so many toys to so many children in one evening?

Or was it that your parents, friends, or others who knew the truth finally dispelled your illusion? Or was it that you grew up Jewish or of another faith and didn't believe in Santa Claus at all, just your other stories?

In Buddhism stories are fine, as long as they lead you to finding the truth. If a preacher or rabbi or swami told you that they magically just put a $20 bill into your purse or wallet, would you believe them? Can you spend it?

If you just hold to the faith that it is there, can you spend it? Sure, you can spend it if it is there, but what if it's not there and you expected it to be there? What a letdown!

What if because you had faith that there was a $20 bill in your wallet or purse, you called up a new friend and asked them to join you on a date to the movies? Well, it would be a bad idea to show up at the movies with your date, open up your wallet or purse, and find out that your faith had misled you.

No, what you should do is open up your wallet or purse and see if in fact there is an extra $20 bill there. Then you don't have to believe in anything or take anything on faith because you know the truth.

Assignment: Superman Dies

The original 1978 film *Superman*, starring Christopher Reeve, tells the story of the greatest superhero of all time. Superman has tremendous strength, x-ray vision, and can fly. He uses his amazing powers to save the world from disaster and apprehend criminals.

Watch *Superman* if you can. In every scene with Superman in his blue and red super suit, pay close attention. Watch closely. Observe the man playing Superman. If you don't have time to watch the film, closely observe the above picture of Superman. As you watch the film or observe the picture, consider the fact that Superman is dead, or, more correctly, Christopher Reeve is dead.

While Superman was his most famous role, Christopher Reeve had performed in hundreds of roles on the stage, TV and cinema. He also wrote, directed and produced films. Christopher Reeve was an accomplished pilot, sailor, SCUBA diver, skier and equestrian.

During an equestrian event in 1995, his Thoroughbred got spooked at a rail jump. He was pitched forward with his hands tangled in the horse's bridle. He landed head first, fracturing the uppermost vertebrae in his spine and was instantly paralyzed from the neck down.

After his accident he fought for greater rights and benefits for paralyzed people. He became the Chairman of the American Paralysis Association and Vice Chairman of the National Organization on Disability. He founded the

Christopher Reeve Foundation and co-founded the Reeve-Irvine Research Center. He successfully lobbied for federal funding on embryonic stem cell research. He also fought on to write a best selling book, *Still Me*, and to direct and act in dozens of films and TV productions. On October 10th 2004, at the age of 52, Christopher Reeve died of a heart attack caused by an infection.

After watching the film, turn to a new page in your Enlightenment Journal and entitle it, "Superman Dies."

If you don't have time to watch the film, instead take a moment to closely observe the picture below.

Consider this vibrant person who had fought his way from humble beginnings to the top of his profession, and then through a devastating accident to great humanitarian accomplishments. Knowing that he is dead now, what reflections of life and death come to mind? What do you know about death after having viewed an energetic snapshot of an accomplished, determined person who once lived and thrived? Write your thoughts in your Enlightenment Journal.

Complete this assignment now. Continue reading when finished.

Assignment: Reflections on My Death

Find the obituary section in your local paper. Take the obituary section with you and go to a cemetery if you can. Take an hour or so for your reflection. Sit down amongst the head stones. Read the obituary section there. Read some of the headstones. Reflect on the people who have died and lay before you or who are remembered in the obituaries.

If you don't have time to go to a cemetery, reflect on what you know about cemeteries or recall a time that you went to a cemetery in the past.

Open your Enlightenment Journal to a new page. Entitle the page "Reflections on My Death." Write your own obituary. If you were to die right now, what would your obituary statement say? Next write your own epitaph. If one of these headstones were yours, what would it say?

Complete this assignment now. Continue reading when finished.

Assignment: Life Near Death

This is a multiple choice assignment. You may choose to do one of the following:

A. Visit with someone who is dying or close to death
B. Watch the film *Letting Go: A Hospice Journey*, directed by Deborah Dickson and Susan Frömke
C. Both A and B

If you know someone who is dying or who is aware that they are close to death, visit with them. If you don't know someone who is close to death, go to a cancer ward, an AIDS hospital, or a convalescent hospital. Visit with someone close to death.

Spend some time with someone who is aware that their life will end soon. Bring your best attention to them. Perhaps come with stories to tell them or pictures from your last vacation. Bring a gift. Flowers are always nice. Share something fun with them!

It is hard for people to muster the courage to do this assignment. You may find that you have strong aversion to doing all the things necessary in order to complete this assignment, but this assignment is worth doing. You're following in the footsteps of the Buddha. The truth that you learn from this assignment is invaluable.

If you find that you are not launching right into choice A, rather than losing momentum and stalling out, choose choice B. *Letting Go* is a powerful documentary which takes an intimate look at three terminally ill patients coping with fear and pain in their last days before death.

Choice C is the most powerful choice. Through your experience visiting someone near death and seeing the documentary, you will learn what Buddha learned when he first encountered someone close to death.

Upon returning from your visit and/or after watching the film, please write about your experiences, observations, and feelings on a new page in your Enlightenment Journal entitled "Life Near Death."

Complete this assignment now. Continue reading when finished.

Assignment: Last Day

If today were your last day alive, what would you do?

If you were to die in 24 hours from this moment, what would you do in your last hours of life?

Would you sleep in and watch TV?

Would you go to work?

Would you spend time with your loved ones?

Would you spend time alone?

Would you meditate?

If you only had this day to live, how would you spend your last day?

Please turn to a new page in your Enlightenment Journal and entitle it, "Last Day." Write down a list of everything you would do if today were your last day of life.

After you plan out what you would ideally do if this were your last day of life, go do it! Live the next 24 hours is if they were you last! Then, write an account of your day.

Complete this assignment now. Continue reading when finished.

The Truth about Death

You can learn about death and life by paying attention to your own experience. Death and life are two sides of the same coin called truth.

Truth exists right now, in this moment. The truth of life can be experienced directly, right now, in this moment. The truth of death can be experienced directly, right now, in this moment. Attention to this moment reveals the truth behind all stories.

The truth about death is that death is not an ending; it is more like a middle. Death is a transition to new life.

Do you remember being born? Do you remember your beginning? No, of course not; consciousness has no beginning. Well, I have good news for you if you fear your death: You won't remember your death either. Consciousness has no ending.

Assignment: Eternality

Now open your Enlightenment Journal and reread "Reflections on a Flower." From reading your own account of connection and awareness of the flower, you can touch a place somewhere beyond life and death, beyond changes, to a place where the flower still blooms.

Reflect on this deeply. Write your experience of this reflection in your Enlightenment Journal on a new page entitled, "Eternality."

Complete this assignment now. Continue reading when finished.

The Conclusion of Suffering

The truth of suffering is the most important thing to realize in beginning the spiritual path. To know that all beings suffer, that you suffer, gives you a reason to seek relief and refuge from suffering.

We tend not to do anything about a problem until it hurts us enough. If after a meal, you start to feel unwell, you know something's wrong. Even though you have discomfort in your tummy, you won't take action to fix it until you start feeling intense nausea. Then you are swift to use the proper medicine.

If after hearing of a friend's good fortune, you start to have some resentful feelings inside, you know that something's wrong. Even though you come to have very jealous thoughts, you will not take action to change until you find yourself striking out at your friend in a jealous rage. Seeing the disastrous outcome of your wayward thoughts, you are swift to control yourself and ask for forgiveness.

"If it ain't broke, don't fix it" is how a lot of us feel. However, if we look inside to see the truth of our lives, we'll often see that there are things that are definitely broke. Our desires, angers, depressions, fears, and jealousies smolder within us as nagging dissatisfactions until they finally burst into the flames of suffering. In knowing the truth of suffering, we learn to extinguish the sparks of passion before they consume us.

"Ignorance is bliss" is what some say. However, being ignorant of the essential truth of life sets you up for untold folly and suffering. It's better to know the truth. It's better to face life as it really is, so that you can become happy in truth.

Becoming aware that our lives are filled with suffering because of our own doing also gives us the knowledge that we can learn how to free ourselves from suffering by our own undoing.

If you're OK with suffering, suffering is OK with you. Whatever you settle for is what you get. If you settle for transient joys and spiritual suffering then you don't need liberation.

Buddha needed a way out. For him the ultimate sorrow of transience greatly outweighed short-term joys. Buddha needed to find the answer to suffering, and in attaining Enlightenment, he did.

The Second Noble Truth

The Second Noble Truth is that there is a cause for our suffering. What causes our suffering is our desire-and-aversion operating system. An operating system for a computer is a fundamental piece of software that tells the computer how to receive, process, and output information, as well as how to manage and run all programs.

Our perception of life primarily results from our fundamental operating system of desires and fears. Our thoughts, words, and actions also result from our desires and fears. Our whole way of being, the activities that we engage in and the friends that we keep all result from our desires and fears.

A student who desires a cigarette so that she can feel more comfortable and relaxed may not realize that actually this same desire will eventually lead her to contracting emphysema and feeling extremely uncomfortable and sick.

If she thought about it with more perspective and squarely faced her desire, she would probably do the opposite of her desire: quit smoking and find a positive way to feel comfortable and relaxed, like meditation.

A man who is constantly oppressed and humiliated by his boss may not realize that he accepts his unhappy situation because he is afraid of being fired and not having a job.

If he thought about it with more perspective and squarely faced his fear, he would probably do the thing that he's afraid of: quit his negative job so that he can find a positive one.

When people approach religion or spirituality, they use the same desire and fear operating system with the same results: suffering. Most people who pray to god ask her for the things they want and ask her to keep away the things they don't want.

We desire to go to heaven and fear hell. People approach Buddhism in the same way, with ideas of gaining and benefiting, but also with fears they hope to avoid.

We are so conditioned by desire and aversion that we suffer greatly. We are trapped into a narrow path of self between what we want and what we fear. Life is broad, but we cannot see beyond the walls of fear and streams of desire that have subtly spread and become our only reality.

Assignment: Desires and Fears of Yesterday

Open your Enlightenment Journal to a new page. Entitle the page, "Desires and Fears of Yesterday."

Create two columns by drawing a line down the center of the page. Label the left column "What I Did Yesterday." Label the right column "Desires/Fears."

In the left column list in single words or short phrases what you did yesterday. After completing the list in the left column, consider each action one at a time.

If the action in the left column originated from or was related to fear or desire, list its relationship in a short phrase in the right column.

Do this assignment with a great degree of self honesty. Give appropriate reflection to each action to see how many important or mundane things that you did yesterday were driven by or related to desires and fears.

Complete this assignment now. Continue reading when finished.

Assignment: What Really Gets My Goat!

Open your Enlightenment Journal to a new page. Entitle the page, "What Really Gets My Goat!"

Create two columns by drawing a line down the center of the page. Label the left column "Mad and Upset." Label the right column "Desires/Fears."

In the left column list in single words or short phrases what makes you mad, what really bothers you. After completing the list in the left column, consider each upsetting thing one at a time.

If the thing in the left column originates from or is related to fear or desire, list its relationship in a short phrase in the right column.

Do this assignment with a great degree of self-honesty. Give appropriate reflection to each item in the mad/upset column to see how many of the things that make you mad and upset derive from or are related to desires and fears.

Complete this assignment now. Continue reading when finished.

Good and Bad Are Ugly

We desire to have what we think is good, and we are averse to what we think is bad. There is an old Taoist story that gives us some insight into our limited dualistic views of good and bad.

It is the story of the farmer and the horse. In Northern China, there was an old farmer whose only possessions were a small shack for a home, an adult son, and a black horse.

One day the farmer's horse ran away. His neighbors consoled him saying, "What a terribly bad thing that happened!"

The farmer scratched his head and said, "Good or bad, who's to say?"

Later that week, his horse returned with a white mare as a companion. His neighbors congratulated him saying, "What a wonderfully good thing that happened!"

The farmer scratched his head and said, "Good or bad, who's to say?"

The farmer's son liked the new white mare very much and rode her everyday. The farmer's neighbors congratulated him and said, "It's so good that your son enjoys riding that horse so much!"

The farmer scratched his head and said, "Good or bad, who's to say?"

One day, the farmer's son took a bad fall when the white mare reared up on her hind legs. His left leg was broken and he needed a crutch to walk. The farmer's neighbors consoled him saying, "What a terribly bad thing that happened!"

The farmer scratched his head and said, "Good or bad, who's to say?"

Then the army came to the small town to recruit all able-bodied men to attempt to defend the province from the overwhelming hordes invading from the West. The farmer's son, being unable to walk without a crutch was not accepted. The farmer's neighbors congratulated him saying, "How wonderful, your son won't have to go off to war!"

The farmer scratched his head and said, "Good or bad, who's to say?"

Who is to say what's good or what's bad? In ignorance, you might think something good is bad. A lot of children think the dentist is bad. In ignorance, you may think something bad is good. Someone might smoke crack because someone tells them it gives you a good feeling.

If you observe good and bad closely and objectively, you'll see that what you consider to be good may also be considered to be bad in another context. Desiring what is good and being adverse to what is bad is an endless loop which does not bring complete satisfaction.

Assignment: Beyond Good and Bad

What things are definitely good to you? What things are definitely bad to you? Write down what you see as good and bad on a new page in your Enlightenment Journal entitled, "Beyond Good and Bad."

After writing your list of what is good and what is bad to you, tempt your imagination to see each concept in its opposite truth. Complete this assignment in the consideration of Chuan Tzu's farmer story. Crack your ideas of good and bad. Be as open-minded as Enlightenment because, "Good or bad, who's to say?"

So if you list "Love and Happiness" as your good concepts, tell your story of opposites like this: "Love is good, but what if a woman loves a man who constantly abuses her?"

"Happiness is good, but what if you are happy at the expense of others? What if the beautiful diamonds that make you so happy have been sold to you by an evil dictator who will use your money to commit genocide?"

If you list "Violence and Depression" as your bad concepts, tell your story of opposites like this: "Violence is bad, but what if a violent man was walking down the street and came across a nun who was being attacked by a gang of thugs? The violent man would have the power to do something amazing—use his violence to save a spiritual sister."

"Depression is bad, but what if, feeling depressed for a long time after a messy divorce, a man begins the study of meditation to find inner peace? What if the man, having learned about the suffering of life through his depression is highly motivated in his spiritual study and attains liberation?"

Complete this assignment now. Continue reading when finished.

Assignment: I Have Attained My Desires

Entitle a new page in your Enlightenment Journal, "I Have Attained My Desires."

Write in your Enlightenment Journal about a time or two when you wanted something really badly and got it. Recall a time when you had a tremendous desire and attained it.

Perhaps it was a girlfriend or boyfriend that you desired. Perhaps it was a bicycle when you were 12 or a car when you were 25. Perhaps you greatly desired an iPod or a PlayStation. Or perhaps you desired a hamburger after spending two weeks visiting your old friend who just became a vegan!

What was it that you desired most? Why did you want it? What did it feel like when you got it? And then what happened after? Did your feelings change? Were you fulfilled and satisfied? Did your desires end?

Complete this assignment now. Continue reading when finished.

Desires Are Endless

Wanting to be happy, you desire this, that, and the other thing. Finding that these don't make you happy enough, you then desire still other things. In this way, desire never stops.

For most people, enough money, the right relationship, the right car, etc. are desirable for happiness. Once we get the things that we thought would make us happy, we find that we still desire improvement in order to be ultimately satisfied.

We think, "Yeah, I made $1 million, and I thought that was a lot at first, but now I need $10 million to be really happy."

We think, "Yeah, I got a Porsche, but I really want to drive a Ferrari!"

We think, "Yeah, I've got the perfect husband, but I wish he'd spend more quality time with me. And stop drinking so much. And stop complaining about my mother's visits. And, and, and..."

There's no end to desire. Nothing truly satisfies us. Once we get something we want, we want something else.

Padmasambhava, the founder of Tibetan Tantra, said, "Beings who are afflicted by ignorance and karma engage in deeds of suffering due to their desire for happiness. Alas for every sentient being who is unskilled in methods!"

When you engage in desire, it has no finish. Desire is endless. Nothing that we desire will make us ultimately happy. Attaining a desire brings a transient joy, which follows the law of changes to become suffering. Attaining a desire brings a short-term balance, but a long-term and ultimate imbalance.

Buddha once remarked, "The rain could turn to gold and still your thirst would not be slacked. Desire is unquenchable. Or it ends in tears even in heaven."

Once upon a time, a greedy and selfish man died. He awoke after his death on a grassy rolling hill under a cloudless sky. To the West he could see the blue ocean. To the East he could see a beautiful waterfall and rainbows.

This was the most beautiful place he could imagine. "I guess I didn't do too badly with my life!" the man thought. "But still, I don't have any place to live here," the man worried. "If only I had a home in this beautiful place."

All of a sudden, right before his eyes, a beautiful mansion appeared! It was the most wonderful home he'd ever seen! The man ran into the home excitedly appraising all the rooms.

"I love my new house!" the man thought. "But it doesn't have any furniture!" he lamented. Just then, the most wonderful, expensive, and tasteful furniture filled every room of his home. The man was thrilled!

After reviewing all of the amazing furniture pieces of his home the man felt hungry. "I'm so hungry!" he thought. "How am I going to find food around here?" Suddenly there was a commotion in the dining room. He walked over to find that a lavish meal of fine foods had appeared on his dining room table. He happily sat down and ate till he was filled and content.

After dining, he felt lonely. "All of this is great!" he thought, "but I wish I could share my life with someone special." At that, there was a knock at the door. To his surprise, a beautiful woman entered his life. She was everything he could ever want for a life partner.

The first few weeks went by quickly. He accumulated many new things: new clothes, fine automobiles, friendly neighbors, and even a friendly pet tiger! All of these things made him happy for a while, but then he needed more things to remain happy.

The next few weeks went by slowly. Although he kept accumulating things at a more rapid pace, he became dissatisfied with them immediately. After a while, nothing at all would really make him happy.

One day he was so dissatisfied, he wished to see whoever was in charge. When the head man appeared, he complained to the head man, "I don't mean to sound ungrateful, but I am just not happy here. It's good to get everything I want and all, but maybe I'm just not supposed to be in heaven!"

The head man responded, "Oh, is that where you thought you were?"

Contrary to what we might think, everything we desire to make us happy will ultimately make us unhappy. Buddha said, "Like a monkey in the forest, you jump from tree to tree, never finding truly satisfying fruit, from life to life never finding peace."

Assignment: The Lifecycle of Desire

Wait until you are really thirsty. Go for a run, play basketball, or just wait until you get really thirsty. When realizing that you have become very thirsty, wait for a few more minutes before drinking water. Be safe about it.

Then when you are really thirsty and you really, really want to drink something, take a moment of recognition of your intense desire to drink. After a moment of reflection on that intense desire, by all means drink! Drink pure water.

Drink all the way! Drink as much as you can. Keep track of how many ounces you drink. Drink until your thirst is quenched. And then keep drinking. Drink until you feel you need no more water. And then keep drinking. Drink until you're full. Drink until you don't want any more water. And then keep drinking. Drink until you absolutely cannot take another sip of water.

As you drink, observe. Observe how in the beginning the water tastes sweet. Observe how the water refreshes and fulfills you. Observe how in the beginning the water seems like the perfect thing, the thing that makes you really happy and content.

Then notice after a short time that you no longer desire the water. You don't need it anymore, and you are OK without it. Then as you keep drinking, you notice that even the taste changes. That which was once so sweet is now not so great.

Notice how drinking becomes more and more difficult. Notice how eventually the taste of the water becomes terrible and how drinking makes you feel worse. Keep drinking until you realize that the last thing you want to do is drink water.

Now you know the lifecycle of desire. The beginning of desire is an intense stream of energy compelling you to get what you need. Upon getting your desire there is some joy. Soon the joy goes away. Eventually suffering is experienced.

In your Enlightenment Journal entitle a new page, "The Lifecycle of Desire." Write the number of ounces you drank in this assignment and any personal observations.

Complete this assignment now. Continue reading when finished.

Wherever You Go, There You Are

A student once approached a Buddhist teacher and said, "I grew up in LA and studied art, but I wasn't happy there, so I moved to New York. New York was fun for a while. I went to a lot of parties and nightclubs. After a while I became unhappy with my dead-end job and clubbing friends. I longed for a formal education and enrolled in a university in Washington DC. Early in my second year at school, I became disenchanted with the idea of taking $40,000 in school loans to learn to be a computer programmer. I didn't like the professors and was unhappy working part-time as a waitress while going to school full-time. Then I met James, the love of my life. I convinced James to leave our school in Washington DC and move with me to Hawaii. Hawaii was fun for a time. We lived in a commune farming papayas. After a few months James broke my heart and married one of the other girls in the commune. Unhappy in the commune with my ex-boyfriend, I moved to San Francisco, where I became interested in Zen Buddhism. I was unhappy with the spiritual community at the Zen Center because they had strict rules about keeping a vegetarian diet and I really like hamburgers. So, I came to study with you. I've enjoyed some of my studies, but I don't really know if your teachings work for me. I've become unhappy again, and I think that if maybe I go back home to Los Angeles, and get back in touch with my roots, that I might find what I'm missing. But a friend told me that he had become very happy by working on a fishing boat in Alaska. So I was thinking that maybe I can become happy if I work on the same fishing boat."

After the long story, the woman asked, "Where do you think I should go to be happy? Should I go back home to LA? Or should I go to the boat in Alaska?"

The teacher answered, "Wherever you go, there you are!"

"What's that mean?" she asked, a bit frustrated.

He answered, "Unhappy here, unhappy there."

"But you don't understand!" she said. "I need to know where to go and what to do to be the happiest. Tell me which way to go to find happiness."

The teacher pointed up into the air and asked, "How about this way?"

She looked up to the bare ceiling of the single story building where he pointed. Standing on the tips of her toes and pounding the low ceiling with her fist, she said, "But there's nothing up there!"

The teacher responded, "Then perhaps you should just look for happiness in the only place that happiness exists: right where you are."

The woman then recognized that the Buddhist teacher had answered the deepest dimension of her question. She reflected deeply on the truth the teacher had shown her and said in the wonder of her realization, "Wherever you go, there you are!" The teacher nodded. She then sat down in meditation and found the happiness she was seeking.

There's nowhere to go and nothing to do that will get you out of this moment. Chasing happiness from here to there means that you are always chasing happiness and never finding it. As Edwin Way Teale said, "If we find no interest in where we are, we are likely to find little interest in where we wish to go." Finding happiness in this moment means that you are no longer seeking happiness and that you are happy.

Buddha said, "Nowhere! Not in the sky, nor in the midst of the sea, nor deep in the mountains, can you hide from your own mischief."

There's nowhere to go to find happiness. Pay attention to right here, right now. Happiness is the natural condition of a still mind. It isn't until we fill our minds with petty thoughts, ideas, and concerns of what we should do to be happy or what we should have to be happy that the stillness of our mind is upset and we find ourselves confused and unhappy. We call these worries and rash schemes our choices.

We consider more choices to be better. We think that lots and lots of choices will give us a greater opportunity to choose the perfect thing, but actually it confuses us from seeing the simple truth of perfection.

One Saturday afternoon, a young man walked into a New York deli. He was getting hungry and wanted to enjoy the 'perfect' sandwich from the renowned eatery.

As soon as he approached the counter, a man wearing a white apron on the other side asked him, "Wha da ya need?" The young man looked up and saw a large hanging chalkboard listing over a hundred breads, cheeses, meats, and much more.

The young man took a couple of minutes to consider all of the different sandwich possibilities to determine what would be the 'perfect' sandwich. As he read down the menu, he thought, "Pastrami might be good! Or what about turkey and avocado?"

Reading on he deliberated, "Tuna salad? No it has mayo. Yuck, I hate mayo!" After carefully considering the complete list of choices again, the young man paused, puckered his lips, tilted his head to the right and then to the left, and then said, "I'll take a pastrami on rye, toasted, with pickles, onions, and lettuce. Extra mustard, salt and pepper. No mayo!"

A couple of minutes later, the man behind the counter handed him a sandwich. After paying for his sandwich and leaving the deli, he bit into his lunch. After several bites, the young man frowned and thought, "I should have had the turkey with avocado. That would have been the perfect sandwich!"

The next day the same young man was helping a friend move into a new apartment. The two of them spent several hours packing, moving furniture, and lifting heavy boxes before they took a break. By the time they were done placing the last box in his friend's new living room, both of them were terribly hungry.

"Want a sandwich?" his friend asked, "I got a couple from the deli before you arrived."

"Yes, please," the young man answered. "I'm famished!"

"I hope tuna fish sandwiches with mayo are OK," his friend said as he tossed him a sandwich. "That's all I got."

The young man nodded, far too hungry to be picky. He enjoyed the tuna fish sandwich tremendously, commenting, "This is the perfect sandwich!"

The sandwich that the young man ordered in the deli was supposed to be the perfect sandwich, but once he started eating it he questioned and found fault with his choice. On the other hand, the sandwich that he ate the next day when there was no choice was as delicious and fulfilling to his panging hunger as any other. He realized that when you're really hungry the perfect sandwich is any sandwich.

An Enlightened Taoist master once said, "When I am hungry, I cook rice. When I am thirsty, I go to the well. When I meditate, I meditate. This is the way of the Tao."

Making the right choices in life is actually very simple. Choose what evolves you. When you are hungry, eat something nutritious. When you are thirsty, drink something hydrating. When you are cold, put on a coat. When you want companionship, seek positive friends. When you want education, go to school. When you want Enlightenment, meditate.

Simplify your life. Attend to what gives you balance. Don't get confused in petty choices. Attend to what brings unity. Don't follow your whims into dissociation. Don't be rash. If you can't tell what is right, then just wait. In moderation and patience, what is right will become self-evident.

The End of Desire

The only escape from the ups and downs of the desires that ultimately bring you no satisfaction and no peace is to stop desire altogether. The Buddha said, "The end of desire is the end of sorrow."

So how then, can we get rid of desire? You can't try to undo desire. A desire to end desire is itself still a desire. Instead, understand that craving itself is what makes you unhappy. Thinking that you need something else in order to be happy is what makes you so unhappy. You are complete now. You don't need anything else to be happy! Seeing that you have everything you need brings you into balance and calm.

Animals don't suffer much from desire. When the sparrow needs food, it finds berries to eat. When the deer needs food, it seeks grasses to eat. When the dolphin needs food, it hunts for fish. Animals don't feel that they need other things to be complete. Animals simply do what they need to do when they need to do it without any existential consternation.

It is quite easy then to be free of desire. Just do what you need to do without expecting to gain anything out of it. That will make you happy. Everything you need to be happy is within you so don't expect to gain happiness outside of yourself. Don't expect to gain happiness by getting something out of life. Don't expect to gain happiness out of wealth or pleasure. Don't expect to gain happiness out of position, respect, or accomplishment. These are powerful streams that will sweep you out of your peace if you play with them in your imagination. Desire, as defined in Buddhism, is a stream of energy that creates diversity by dividing unity into a selfish awareness of separativity. Each desire we have is a further definition of a limited, lacking self.

Out of ignorance we think attaining certain desires will make us happy, but all desires serve to bring us out of balance and happiness. Desire is the attempt of the fearful, deluded ego to achieve happiness. Because of your clinging to a limited sense of self, you misinterpret what will bring you true happiness. Unable to see what brings unity, you embrace short-term joys that cause you long-term imbalance and unhappiness.

Instead, trust life. Trust that you'll get what you need. You have so far, and not because of your doing, but because of life's granting. Life grants the sow green pastures. Life grants the hawk its prey. Life will sustain you, and your desires will only make you unhappy.

So then let go of desire. Release the powerful stream. It's so much easier to be out of that motion, free and still. To have desires is so much work. It is so absorbing of attention and limiting of awareness. Each desire you have is a heavy, heavy burden. So let go of your burdens. Buddha said, "It is not iron that imprisons you. Nor rope, nor wood. But the pleasure you take in gold and jewels, sons and wives. Soft fetters, yet they hold you down."

Fear

Fear keeps us agitated and frozen. It stifles us and limits us. The lack of fear feels great! When we are unhindered by fear, we are in balance with the forces of life and can take advantage of new opportunities for advancement.

In the dark a rustling noise to our left keeps us constantly uneasy. A long snake before us keeps us from moving. In the light, we see that on our left, the wind blows amongst rose bushes. The rustling sound adds to the beauty. In the light we can see that there is no snake before us, but a walking staff to help us journey forth.

On the first day of his first year of high school, a young man, very excited about being in a new larger school, approached a group of older popular boys. He walked over to the group and said, "Hi, my name is Ned Ryerson. Would you like to be friends?"

The group of boys began to howl with laughter. One of the older boys stepped forward and said, "No, geek! We don't want to be your friend! You're such a loser!"

The other boys began to taunt him, chanting, "Loser! Loser! Loser!"

Many of the boys and girls in the schoolyard looked on giggling as the freshman was humiliated by the older boys. Finally one of the older boys pushed the young man into a nearby garbage can. The garbage can fell over and the young man lay face down in sticky lunchtime trash. The older boys again howled with laughter.

From that day on the young man kept to himself. He no longer approached others in friendship and was always on guard when others approached him. Every day during lunchtime he would read books alone in the library.

Some years later, while in college, the young man became a serious and well read student of Buddhism. One day as he finished a group meditation session at the meditation hall, his Buddhist teacher invited him over for a chat.

His teacher said, "You are an exemplary student! I would like to meet with you and a few of your friends from the university to discuss the history of Buddhism as a vehicle of higher learning."

The young man replied, "I don't have any friends at the university."

The teacher asked, "Now why is that?"

The young man replied, "Well, uh, I don't really know how to make friends. Other people seem to be so different. They seem to be into different things. That's why I got into Buddhism."

"I see," said the Buddhist teacher, "so, I will meet with you and let's say ten of your friends next week at this time!"

The young man shook his head saying, "No, I told you that I don't have any friends and don't know how..."

His teacher interrupted, "Don't argue your fears to me. I understand that you're afraid. Rather, realize that your fears are barriers to your own true nature." The young man then reflected on his teacher's lesson and realized how his fears limited him and had shaped his life. He bowed to his teacher.

The next week, the young man appeared for his meeting with his Buddhist teacher. The young man brought 12 friends from the university. After a stimulating discussion, many of them decided to stay for a group meditation session with the other students of the meditation hall.

Later, the teacher asked, "So, how did you make these new friends?"

"I met them all by putting up posters and handing out flyers around campus," the young man answered. He went on, "The subject was so interesting to me, I thought others might be of like mind. We had a pre-meeting yesterday so that I could explain to them your background and what a meeting with you is like. We all got along very well and some of my new friends have invited me to other educational and social events at school."

The Buddhist teacher said, "See, when you get fear out of the way, the very things you feared can end up being good friends!"

The Buddha said, "In his fear a man may shelter in the mountains or forests, in the groves of sacred trees or in the shrines, but how can he hide from his sorrow? There are no fears for the one whose thoughts are untroubled, whose mind is not confused, who ceases to think of good and bad, who is aware."

Once Dawn, a long-time friend of a Buddhist practitioner named Mary, came to Mary for some spiritual advice for a problem she called "illogical."

"Tell me Dawn," Mary said, "what's your illogical problem?"

Dawn burst into tears saying, "It's Brad!" Brad was her boyfriend of two years.

"Has Brad done something to make you so upset?" Mary asked.

"No, not at all!" Dawn said. Holding back her tears now she repeated, "It's so illogical!"

"Feelings don't have to be logical to be real," Mary said, "Something real causes your suffering. Feelings reach closer to our spirit than logic. Trust your feelings. Explain your feelings about Brad to me and I bet we'll find a way out of your sorrow!"

Dawn nodded and said, "Brad is such a perfect guy! I mean, I couldn't imagine a more perfect guy. Our relationship is really good. It's the best relationship I've ever had! He's caring and honest. He's always supportive of me!" Dawn paused and began to weep again softly. Then she said, "I just don't know if I'm good enough for him. I don't know if I'm pretty enough or smart enough!"

"But you've been good enough, pretty enough, and smart enough so far for two years now," Mary said.

"Yeah, but I'm still afraid of losing him! OK?" Dawn nearly shouted.

"OK," Mary answered. "It looks like you've just pointed to the real problem: your fear. You fear losing Brad."

These words struck Dawn as true. Mary asked, "Reflect on this. Call it out. Does your illogical suffering have to do with anything else besides fear?"

Dawn thought about it for a long time and answered, "No. It's true, I am afraid of losing Brad. What am I to do? How do I move beyond my fear?"

"If you want to move beyond your fear of losing Brad," Mary answered, "just be grateful for the time that you do have together and be OK with the fact that someday, by his choice, by your choice, or by death you will definitely lose Brad. Your fear of losing what you're attached to will drive you to misery unless you face your fears and overcome them in your own mind."

Dawn took Mary's advice to heart. In time she let go of her fears and unabashedly enjoyed her relationship with Brad.

The Buddha said, "From cravings and attachments to pleasures and lusts grow grief and fear. Like nothing lest you lose it. Go beyond likes and dislikes. What gives you pleasure will change. And the fear of the change causes suffering."

Another time, a distressed woman approached a Buddhist teacher in tears. The teacher asked, "What is it that causes you so much sorrow?"

After taking a moment to compose herself, the woman said, "I'm afraid to love again. The first man I loved ended up cheating on me. That hurt so bad that I never wanted to feel that way again. I searched for two years for a man who I could trust; a man I knew would not cheat on me. I met Rick, and we were married for over ten years until his death."

She continued, "His death hurt me so much that I never wanted to feel that way again. So I decided that love just has too much potential for hurt. My first love crushed my heart, and my second love died, leaving me alone and in even more pain."

She paused for a moment and said, "But now, there is a special man, that I've been friends with for some time. He says that he loves me and wants to be with me. I want to love him, but I'm afraid because I've been hurt so badly in the past. What should I do?"

The teacher answered, "Have the courage to love again. Never let your fear of past pain stop you from loving. Love is truth, love is union. Never let fears stop love. Always gain courage from love to overcome fears."

The woman said, "OK, I want to do it! I want to love again, but I still have so much fear. How do I love when I have so much fear to love? How do I gain courage from love?"

The teacher answered, "By recognizing the truth of love and following it no matter what. When you see the truth and the truth is your resolve, you will know truth and love without a doubt. Courage does not mean the lack of fear. It means that you do what is conducive to truth and love even in the face of your greatest fears. Buddhists have tremendous courage. That's why it is said that Buddhists are spiritual warriors. Buddhists courageously face their fears in order to know truth and love. Buddhists face the darkness of the self to know Enlightenment. Buddhists know the secret to love. That is, to love freely. Love is free! And love is a freedom that you must exercise regularly!"

In hearing these words, the woman saw the truth of her love. Seeing the truth of her love, she gained the courage to love again.

Because love is so fantastic, out of the fear of losing something so wonderful, most people affix love to the objects that have inspired them to ascend into an awareness of love.

Affixing love immediately binds love in conditions so that love is no longer free. Affixing love is the beginning of attachment. Once attachments are created, love gets covered over by self-definitions and expectations.

These mixed expressions of love and self-attachments are what people experience commonly in their relationships. It starts with an innocent love, and then it changes into "our love," and then many other associated definitions that finally amount to "our current condition" of transient joys and pains. Because of fear, our love and our hate can exist in a relationship at the same time.

Becoming fearless extricates you from the folly of the ego's suffocating grip on love. Being fearless doesn't mean that you are reckless or cavalier with your life or your love. It means just the opposite. When you are beyond fear you are vigilant and apprehend information about situations that will help you preserve your life, increase your happiness and evolve your consciousness.

On one occasion at an inner city meditation center a student asked a Buddhist teacher about fear. He said, "Last year, I saw a man pull out a pistol. He started shooting it in the air. Everyone took cover, but I was too afraid to even move. Is fear of a gun bad?"

The teacher asked him if he had ever been in any other life-threatening situation. He immediately told his teacher about a time when he was camping and a poisonous rattlesnake lunged at him. "If I hadn't been quick on my feet, I'd have been done in for sure!"

The teacher then asked, "Are you afraid of snakes?"

He answered, "No. I mean, I don't want them to bite me, but they don't really freak me out all that much."

The teacher said, "Well, that shows you something! In one situation you faced a gun that could kill you and you were unable to act to save yourself. You were just lucky that you weren't killed. In another situation you faced a poisonous snake that could kill you and you were swift to stay clear of its imminent attack."

He nodded in agreement. The teacher continued, "This shows you that yes, a fear of guns is not beneficial to you because it paralyzes you from taking action to keep yourself safe from harm. You should overcome your fear of guns and acknowledge them in the same way that you respect the deadliness of a rattlesnake. They are things that require your full and active attention in dealing with."

"OK! How do I overcome my fear for guns? Should I go shoot guns? Or should I hang around bad neighborhoods where people might pull guns on me?"

"Heavens, no! Never put yourself in harm's way to learn about a fear. You just have to seriously reflect on what makes you afraid. Open your journal and write down your fears about guns in detail. Reflect on your fears of guns as well as your intelligent apprehension of the deadliness of rattlesnakes. With a clear mind from your meditation you'll be able to see where your fears come from and how to address them. Write and reflect, see the truth for yourself."

Assignment: What I'm Afraid Of

Turn to a new page in your Enlightenment Journal and entitle the page, "What I'm Afraid Of."

Now consider your fears. What are you afraid of? What causes you fear? Write down your fears. List out all of your fears and describe them. Then rank your top five fears.

Complete this assignment now. Continue reading when finished.

Assignment: My Greatest Fearful Experiences

Turn to a new page in your Enlightenment Journal and entitle the page, "My Greatest Fearful Experiences."

Now consider your experiences with fear in the past. What was the most frightening experience you've ever had? Write down one or more of your experiences and what you've learned from them.

Complete this assignment now. Continue reading when finished.

Assignment: Fears That Stop Me

Turn to a new page in your Enlightenment Journal and entitle the page, "Fears That Stop Me." Consider whether fear stops you from reaching your dreams. Think of one or a few life goals. What are the fears that are associated with these goals?

Write the goals and fears in your Enlightenment Journal. Also write in depth about how you can overcome these fears in achieving your goals.
Complete this assignment now. Continue reading when finished.

Assignment: Fear Flick

It is arguable that the movie "The Shining" is the scariest horror film of all time! Watch "The Shining" or another supernatural horror film that you think may be even more frightening.

Turn to a new page in your Enlightenment Journal and entitle the page, "Fear Flick." Write an entry about the film in your Enlightenment Journal. How did you feel watching the movie? What can you learn about the horrific situations in the movie? What did you learn about your fear from watching the film?

Complete this assignment now. Continue reading when finished.

Assignment: Overcoming Fear

Turn to a new page in your Enlightenment Journal and entitle it "Overcoming Fear." Consider the fears you've identified in the previous assignments. Can you overcome these fears?

Face your fears. Intend to overcome your fears. Spend a day facing and overcoming your fears. Begin with your smallest fears. Even overcoming one small fear is a great success. After you overcome the small fears, you will learn that all fears are the same in nature and that you can succeed in overcoming your top five greatest fears.

Do this safely! Remember, never put yourself in harm's way to learn about fear. You just have to reflect seriously on what makes you afraid. If you can safely engage in an act that causes you fear, then I recommend you do it! For example, if you are afraid of speaking in public, volunteer to give a presentation at your school or work. If making new friends causes you fear, simply approach others at school or work in a friendly way with a smile. Write an Enlightenment Journal entry about your experience.

Complete this assignment now. Continue reading when finished.

The Third Noble Truth

The Third Noble Truth is that there is an end to suffering. Just as the winter yields to the spring, so does suffering yield its grasp of sorrow. That which arises also ceases.

Helen Keller observed, "Although the world is full of suffering, it is also filled with the overcoming of it." Conditions and objects which cause suffering are also subject to the law of changes. It is wise then, even in the midst of suffering, to direct your mind to truth. Your suffering will end in its time and your awareness of truth will be forever.

The Buddha said, "Set your heart on doing good. Do it over and over again. And you will be filled with joy. Before the newly poured milk curdles, it takes time for it to turn. Before the fruit of virtue is tasted and known, it takes time to ripen."

Wrongdoers may see happiness from their bad deeds for a time, but when the karmas of wrong action ripen, the wrongdoers see only misery and darkness. A good person may suffer for a time, but when her goodness blossoms, the good person only sees truth and light.

The Buddha said that the world is on fire and that we are asleep. It is as if we are frogs sitting in a pan of lukewarm water over a slowly growing fire. The rise in temperature is slow and gradual. The changes in increasing heat are subtle. Under these circumstances a frog would stay in the water until cooked dead. If the temperature changes were more drastic, the frog would jump out of the pan to safety. Instead, unaware that the small uncomfortable changes can lead to peril, the frog stays in an ever-worsening situation.

If we observe subtle patterns, we can extricate ourselves from a bad situation before it consumes us. We can tell when something is headed in an unhealthy direction and make a course correction. With awareness of what is going on, and a desire for truth, we can follow the appropriate steps to leap out of conditions of suffering.

When I was ten, I started neglecting my mother's directions to brush my teeth before going to bed. It was a big chore when I was so tired. Soon, it became my habit to skip this obligation. Not long after a successful yield on Halloween night, one of my teeth started hurting. Yet I went on eating candy and practicing minimal oral hygiene.

One day, my mother told me that it was time for my visit to the dentist. I had already had a cavity or two in my time, and I was not pleased by this news, owing to the fact that I had a sharp pain in a molar. The fateful day came and I sat back in the dental chair saying, "Ah." After my dentist's initial inspection, he shook his head, and said, "Looks like we've got six cavities."

That was one of the most painful days of my life. He gave me two shots of Novocain to no avail. While he was drilling two of my molars I felt the most excruciating pain. I cried and shook. I pushed his hands away and at one point climbed off of the chair and attempted to flee the room. All of my crying and pushing ended up being useless. My friendly-mannered dentist just firmly held me down and drilled away.

After that day, I brushed and flossed in the morning, before bed, and after all sugary snacks with the greatest of discipline. I went over my dentist's comic book-like pamphlet on proper brushing techniques for children called "Super Brush and Wonder Floss" daily. I even brushed a loose tooth after it came out, before I handed it over to the tooth fairy. I was dead set on not suffering the drill again!

Through an understanding of what is proper and by suffering the results of improper attention to what is proper, we learn that there's a reason to do the right thing. Once we're savvy to this fact, we then just have to learn how to do the right thing properly.

Assignment: What I Learned to End Suffering

What valuable lessons have you learned from suffering? Entitle a new page in your Enlightenment Journal, "What I Learned to End Suffering."

Enter a story or two about how you experienced suffering of some sort due to ignorance or fear, and then how you learned what to do in order to end the suffering.

Complete this assignment now. Continue reading when finished.

The Fourth Noble Truth

The Fourth Noble Truth is that the teachings of Enlightenment are the way out of suffering. Just as you can use awareness and knowledge to overcome a particular situation or object of suffering, as you experienced in the Third Noble Truth, you can use awareness and knowledge to overcome the source of all suffering.

The Upanishads, a book of ancient teachings of Enlightenment from India, says, "Rare it is to hear of the teachings of Enlightenment. Even more rare it is to receive the teachings of Enlightenment. And most rare is the one who practices the teachings of Enlightenment."

Buddha's teachings of Enlightenment are called the Eightfold Path. I also call it the Right Stuff! The Eightfold Path consists of:

1. Right meditation
2. Right mindfulness
3. Right view
4. Right intent
5. Right speech
6. Right action
7. Right job
8. Right effort

By using the word "right" Buddha was not intending an inference of there being a "wrong." In this world we are inclined to see things as pairs of opposites. We see good and bad, right and wrong, beautiful and ugly, life and death.

A self that is defined by limitation cannot perceive in wholeness, so must divide the whole into dual and opposite extremes. A dualistic view favors awareness of one side of life and shuns the other side of life. A dualistic view cannot embrace all of life. A dualistic view of life is an incomplete view of life. What the Buddha meant by "right" is that which is proper, that which aids your evolution, that which is conducive to truth and awakening.

When the Buddha spoke of the pathway to Enlightenment he said, "When I pulled out sorrow's shaft, I showed you the way. It is you who must make the effort. The masters only point the way. Give yourself to the journey."

To study the Eightfold Path is to study the Buddha's prescription for Enlightenment. With the realizations of the Four Noble Truths, it's possible to follow the Eightfold Path to attain liberation. In this study you will uncover the reality of these precious teachings in your life.

Right Meditation

The study of meditation is a proper beginning. Meditation is the foundation of all Buddhist practice. The spiritual experience in any practice or religion is ultimately meditation. Meditation is the greatest aid to your Enlightenment. Meditation is the essence of all practice.

Right meditation is stopping thought. If you stop thinking, that's meditation! The primary instruction for meditation is that simple: stop thought!

More importantly for most people is to learn what meditation is not. Meditation is not spacing out. It's not sleeping. It's not being dissociated so that your awareness level descends to a place lacking cognition of thought. Meditation is also not day dreaming or astral traveling.

Right meditation is being awake and aware. Right meditation is engaging the moment and stopping thought completely. That's all there is to it. There are many more things that you can say about meditation, but you primarily learn how to do right meditation by doing it.

Assignment: My Meditation Experience

So let's give it a try now. Sit up nice and straight. Stop thought for about five minutes. Use a clock or watch to check the time if you'd like. After this period of meditation, write in your Enlightenment Journal about your experience. Entitle a new page in your Enlightenment Journal, "My Meditation Experience."

If you've had any thoughts or feelings during the meditation write everything you had thought and felt for those five minutes in detail. As well, if you've had any subtle feelings or awarenesses, write about them in detail. Write in detail about your whole meditation experience.

Complete this assignment now. Continue reading when finished.

Post Assignment

When you're new to meditation you learn a really important thing from this Assignment: you are always thinking and it's really hard to try to stop thinking. The quantity of thoughts that you find yourself having in five minutes could be surprising. This is a good beginning! You are learning about what's going on in your mind. This is a vital step in expanding your awareness. With more learning you can master what's going on in your mind and experience the purity of your luminous spirit unclouded by the distraction of thoughts.

Meditation is kind of hard to do in the beginning. Like learning a language, it takes time to become fluent. But hang in there. Meditation is a good language to know, because meditation is the language of Enlightenment!

Although your first attempts at consciously stopping your thoughts and ascending to a higher state of awareness may not be as good as you'd wish, many people who are interested in learning meditation have naturally experienced meditation before.

Have you ever watched a sunset, sat by the ocean, or taken a walk in the forest and felt complete inner peace and well-being? Have you ever listened to beautiful music and felt that life was big and filled with possibilities for happiness? Have you ever been alone and just felt quiet and connected to the universe? These are experiences of meditation.

There are times where by the grace of eternity we experience meditation. It may happen in nature or perhaps in listening to timeless music. When it happens, we are filled with joy and light. When it happens, we are empty of thoughts.

If you've experienced meditation naturally, the power, love and wisdom that you felt may be the reason that you are drawn to a formal study. Right meditation is the discipline of invoking the experiences of Enlightenment and the cessation of thoughts.

Meditation is a period of time set aside every day to practice stilling the mind. Meditation helps you become calm and balanced. It is a way for you to cultivate a connection to the eternal side of being. In the beginning of meditation practice, we work on slowing down our thoughts. After some practice, we learn to stop thought completely. When you become adept in meditation, you learn to enter the pinnacle state of meditation called Samadhi. In Samadhi the mind is perfectly merged with Nirvana, the essence of life.

Meditation recharges you and brings you into bright states of consciousness. It brings clarity of mind and awakens your intuition. Meditation makes you happy and bright. It also empowers you to accomplish things in your daily life by connecting you to the power of the universe. Eventually, dedicated meditation practice leads to Enlightenment. Each meditation session, including your first meditation, brings you into a greater condition of light. Each meditation session brings you closer to Enlightenment.

In the early Tibetan Mystery Schools, the Enlightened masters taught, "Meditation is the bridge between this and all other levels of consciousness. Practicing meditation makes you aware of your eternally Enlightened nature. By practicing meditation you will come to see that the true nature of the real you, the body of light, is everlasting bliss!"

Many styles of meditation practice exist today. They generally involve focusing on energy centers in the body, concentrating on a picture or image, chanting, or breathing exercises. Regardless of the style, they all share a common goal: stopping thought. While the forms of meditation vary, they all use a point of focus to help you stop your thoughts. In general, the technique for meditation is this: Draw all of your thoughts into one focus and be freed of all thoughts. When our thoughts stop, we can connect to worlds of light, power, wisdom, and pure consciousness.

You will find that each meditation session brings a little more clarity and power into your life. The most important things are perseverance in your practice and the ability to never judge your meditation. Meditation takes practice, so don't expect too much too soon. If you find your mind wandering away from your meditation, do not get frustrated. Simply bring your mind gently back to the technique. Trust yourself. With earnest effort you can master meditation.

It is helpful to take a shower or wash your hands and face prior to each meditation session. Water helps refresh you. Water also neutralizes heavy energies that may accumulate in your aura, the subtle-physical body of energy that surrounds and encompasses your physical body.

You may want to set aside a special place in your room that you only use for meditation. Also, it's a good idea not to eat too much before you meditate, or you will feel heavy and tired.

It is important to keep your back straight during meditation, whether you are sitting on the floor or in a chair. Energy flows up the spine, so it is important to create a straight pathway for it.

At the end of a meditation session, bow in gratitude and offer your meditation back to the universe. This is a gesture of humility and appreciation for life.

Now let's learn chakra meditation, the principal form of meditation in Buddhist mysticism. Chakra meditation involves concentrating on energy centers, called chakras, which are found in the aura, or subtle-physical body.

These energy centers are located along a nonphysical energetic meridian called the sushumna. The sushumna in the subtle-physical body corresponds to the spinal column in the physical body. The sushumna begins at the base of the spine and ends at the "third eye," between the eyebrows and a little above.

Seven primary chakras are found at different points along the sushumna. Kundalini, also called chi or prana, is a refined spiritual energy that resides at the base of the spine in the first chakra. During chakra meditation, the kundalini energy is pulled from the first chakra up through the sushumna to the third eye in the area of the forehead where the sushumna ends.

In very advanced meditation practice, when a great deal of energy is generated and held in the third eye, the energy can leap from the third eye to the seventh chakra. The seventh chakra is called the "crown" chakra or the "thousand petaled lotus of light." The seventh chakra sits just above the sushumna, several inches above the top of the head. When the kundalini leaps to the crown chakra, the state of Samadhi occurs in which one is merged with eternity.

When a practitioner enters into Samadhi, he or she has entered into the first stages of Enlightenment. Entering into Samadhi repeatedly will eventually lead a practitioner to a state of complete awareness, in which that person has actually become one with Enlightenment itself.

In chakra meditation, we focus on three of the seven primary energy centers. By "focus," I mean that we place our attention on the areas of the body which correspond with each chakra, one at a time. We concentrate on the energy center, thereby activating it and releasing its energy. Sometimes it is helpful to place your fingers gently on each center as you meditate to help you feel where they are. Eventually, you will naturally feel the energy centers in your body.

We start with the third chakra, the "navel" or "power" center, which is approximately two inches below the navel. By meditating here, the first three centers are activated and great power is released into your being. This energy gives you the ability to accomplish physical things. This is the center for willpower and strength. This affords you a spiritual power to rise above difficulties and be happy. This chakra is the primary doorway to Enlightenment in mysticism.

We then move to the fourth chakra, the "heart" center. This center is located in the center of the chest and in the general area of the heart. This is the center for love, balance, and happiness.

Finally, we focus on the sixth chakra, the "third eye." This chakra is located in the center of the forehead between the eyebrows and slightly above them. This is the center for wisdom, psychic seeing, and dreaming.

It is generally a good idea to spend an equal amount of time meditating on each chakra. If you meditate for 15 minutes, spend five minutes focusing on each chakra. Likewise, if you meditate for an hour, spend 20 minutes concentrating on each chakra. By practicing chakra meditation in this way, you will bring power, balance and wisdom into your life.

If you are new to meditation, start by meditating for 15 minutes per session. After a few months, when you are comfortable meditating for 15 minutes, increase your meditation sessions to 30 minutes. When you are comfortable meditating for 30 minutes, increase your meditation sessions to 45 minutes. When you are comfortable with 45 minutes, increase your meditation sessions to a full hour.

Within a year of practice you should be able to meditate comfortably for one hour. Once you've reached the ability to practice meditation for one hour, there is no need to increase the period of time. At this point you should work on stopping thought and becoming as still as possible for the entire period.

Practice meditation twice per day. It is very beneficial to meditate in the morning. As soon as you wake up, take a shower, have some coffee or tea if you have to, and then meditate. In the morning your mind is most still as you emerge from sleep. Don't engage in conversations, emails, or breakfast. Meditate before you get caught up in the affairs of the day. Meditating in the morning energizes you to be clear and powerful in all the activities of your day.

It is also very beneficial to meditate in the evening. It's a good idea to shower and meditate right before going to bed. Evening meditation ends your day in a powerful reflection of light. Meditating before going to bed also helps you to be relaxed and peaceful so that your sleep is restful and recuperative. Evening meditation also has a very positive effect on dreaming.

Assignment: My Second Step in Meditation

Now we'll practice meditation one more time. With these additional instructions you'll find it easier to be more quiet and more empty of thoughts. This meditation will be more still and bright.

Begin by sitting up straight. Focus on your navel chakra. Hold your finger lightly touching the area of your navel. Count 20 slow breaths as you focus on the navel center. Inhale, exhale, one, inhale, exhale, two.

After reaching 20 deep breaths, bring the focus to your heart chakra. Hold your finger lightly touching the area of your heart. Count 20 slow breaths as you focus on the heart center. After reaching 20 deep breaths, bring the focus to your third eye. Hold your finger lightly touching the area of your third eye. Count 20 slow breaths as you focus on the third eye.

Entitle a new page in your Enlightenment Journal, "My Second Step in Meditation." If you had any thoughts during the meditation write everything you thought in detail. Also if you've had any subtle feelings or awarenesses write about them in detail.

You will notice that you have fewer thoughts and more subtle and energetic feelings. This is the path to the cessation of thought and expanded subtle awareness. You've made a step into the light!

Complete this assignment now. Continue reading when finished.

Assignment: Daily Meditation Practice

Begin a daily meditation practice. Meditation is the foundation of Buddhist practice. Meditation gives you the power and clarity to progress on the spiritual path.

At least for the period of time that you continue to read this book, meditate twice per day every day.

Please continue reading on.

Right Mindfulness

Post Assignment

Right mindfulness is a practice of constantly grooming your mind of negative thoughts and emotions. Right mindfulness is constantly holding positive thoughts that serve truth and awakening in your mind. It is choosing in every moment to be positive about life.

Right mindfulness leads to the mastery of your mind. Mastery of the mind means that you control the dark, harmful tendencies of thought that create sorrows for yourself and others. Mastery of the mind means that you only hold the most expansive, bright, and grounded thoughts in any difficult or mundane situation.

The Buddha said, "As the fletcher whittles and makes straight his arrows, so the master directs his straying thoughts."

Mindfulness is based on the Buddhist principle that we are what we think. The mind does not have a particular shape or form. In actuality, the mind is as fluid as water. The mind takes whatever form you put it into. Just as water poured from a tall thin glass into a short wide mug changes into the form of the mug, the mind takes the form of your mental and emotional attitudes. The thoughts and feelings you allow to run through your attention will determine the shape of your mind.

So if you focus on unhappy and negative things, you will become unhappy and negative. On the other hand if you focus on happy and positive things, you will become happy and positive.

Post Assignment

Right mindfulness is taking responsibility for your mind. It is owning up to the truth that happiness is something you choose. Right mindfulness is the acknowledgment that what you think and what you feel is solely up to your discretion. The decision to direct your thoughts and feelings toward that which is positive, healthy, and true is up to you.

Most people act as if they are a leaf in the wind. Their happiness is completely dependent on what happens to them. Which way the wind blows determines which way their mind thinks. One who practices right mindfulness is as a stone in the wind. Though the transient winds of life blow strong, the stone is not moved. Right mindfulness is taking control of your life by taking control of your thoughts.

Some people judge that forcing yourself to think positively is hypocritical and not in line with truth. They think that when something bad happens, if they act positive and happy in response to it, that they would be fooling themselves and not being real about life. They think that pretending to be positive in the face of adversity would be denying the truth, acting superficial, and just being fake.

While being overly altruistic and idealistic can be out of balance with truth, practicing right mindfulness is wise and mature in truth. If you were crippled in a car accident and bound to a wheelchair for life it would be silly to think, "OK, I bet that I'll be back up on my feet in no time flat!" If you were practicing right mindfulness you would think rather, "I'm lucky to be alive. Although I've lost the use of my legs, there are still so many things I can do. I've always wanted to take up painting! I can learn computer science to have a good job! And I can keep practicing meditation!"

Right mindfulness is not fanciful thoughts that are out of line with truth. Right mindfulness is positive thoughts that are congruent with truth and aid awakening. Right mindfulness is keeping the perspective of Enlightenment in the face of any difficulty. If you are aligned with ultimate truth nothing is so bad. In actuality what we normally call "bad" is something that compels us to contemplate a deeper understanding of truth. With right mindfulness, bad things give us an opportunity to see not only new good things, but the perfection of truth itself.

Assignment: How Bad Is Bad?

Entitle a new page in your Enlightenment Journal, "How Bad Is Bad?"

Continuing on from the consideration of the previous assignment, in reflecting on the fact that you have less than six months to live, how bad is the previous news that you were fired or expelled?

What are your thoughts and feelings about this reflection?

Complete this assignment now. Continue reading when finished.

Post Assignment

The truth is always positive, bright, and wholesome. Thoughts that are against a true, wholesome view are hypocritical. Transient thoughts with little vision create darkness. Open-minded thoughts with vast perspective create light.

In much the same way that your body needs to work out in order to become strong, your mind is like a muscle: you have to work it out in order to strengthen it! Eliminating negative thoughts and emotions from your mind is like physical exercise, a healthy good habit!

Eventually, you will find that you feel better and happier throughout the day, because you will not be allowing yourself to be brought down by any negativity you may encounter. Then at the end of the day, you will discover that you have more energy for the evening.

The Buddha said, "Your worst enemy cannot harm you as much as your own thoughts unguarded. But once mastered, no one can help you as much."

Assignment: Now How Bad Is It Really?

Again, continuing on from the consideration of the previous assignment, finally let's say that you get a last phone call. It is your doctor again. He apologizes, saying that the "brain cloud" diagnosis was not for you. It was actually for a 108-year-old Eskimo named Sergey Mohammad Velasquez. Your doctor explains that his secretary had confused your names and accidentally put your phone number on the file.

Entitle a new page in your Enlightenment Journal, "Now How Bad Is It Really?" Now write in your Enlightenment Journal how the loss of your livelihood or education makes you feel. What are your thoughts and feelings? Are they different in light of being free from your "brain cloud"?

Complete this assignment now. Continue reading when finished.

Assignment: An Hour of Mindfulness

Spend the next hour being mindful of your thoughts. Go about whatever activities you need to. Have dinner with your family, go shopping at the supermarket, or drive to work. Whatever you have to do in the next hour, do it while practicing mindfulness. Watch your mind carefully. See what you're thinking in any activity.

After spending an hour practicing mindfulness, open a new page in your Enlightenment Journal and entitle it, "An Hour of Mindfulness."

Write about your experience. What did you notice about your thoughts? Was it difficult to watch your thoughts? What did you think?

Complete this assignment now. Continue reading when finished.

Right View

No particular view is right view. A right view is a fluid view. It is not a frozen conceptual view. A right view sets no limits on life. From the moment we were born, we started building a mental model of the world. This description of the world included what is good and bad, what food we like, who we are, and everything else.

When we gained more information, we added this information to our existing model. We added religious stories, societal stories, concepts of what men and women should do, and everything that is our description of the world today.

Our model contains some very useful information, like how to cross the street and how to get a job. This model is useful in a lot of ways but cannot be relied on to bring us truth and happiness.

Your model of the world can be likened to a model of a building. A building model describes what a building is like. It describes the building's form and structure, its size and dimensions. A building's model describes the building perfectly in an important way so that the building can be constructed using the model. A building's model is the building, but on a much more limited and smaller scale.

However, a building is much more than its model! A building is the reality that the model tries to describe. If you are only aware of the model of the building, you will never know what it feels like to be in the building. A building is a space you experience, a space that no model can describe.

It is because we rely on our model of the world to describe the world completely that we fall into an incorrect view of all of life. Any description of life would fall short of describing all of life. Models and descriptions are helpful, but we must rely on a whole view of life itself, a right view to see truth and find happiness.

Conceptual models freeze us into an inflexible frame for seeing life. Conceptual modeling is what creates existential angst. In any given circumstance we may know exactly what's going on and how we feel about it, yet simultaneously experience a deeper discord. Our happiness is often suffocated, constricted by our own outlook.

Let's talk about taxes and the weather. When it's time to fill out IRS income tax return forms, one may think, "What a bothersome chore!" Most people have a fixed concept that doing taxes equals stress. On the other hand, when it is 72°, the sun is out, and there are no clouds in the sky, one may think, "This is great weather!" Most people have a fixed concept that good weather equals happiness.

Why, even the meteorologist on TV will say, "It's a beautiful day!" Anyone you pass on the street and mention the weather to will give a favorable and positive response, even in a busy city. For many people the concept of good weather triggers other pleasant related thoughts about going to the beach, hiking in the woods, or having a barbecue.

Now, if someone had to do their taxes on a day when there is great weather, they may feel very unhappy. They know that doing taxes gives them some stress and upsets them a little bit, but a deeper, more intangible unhappiness arises. This mysterious dismay arises because their sadness on a sunny day is in conflict with their model of life.

This conflict causes more unhappiness than just doing taxes alone. They become sad and can't quite put their finger on why they are so sad. Life seems so confusing at these times. They understand the conditions of their situation, but don't know why it is so upsetting. Ultimately their great dissatisfaction arises from their own conflicting model of existence. Their frozen views don't make sense. Their frozen views clash with reality. Their frozen views drive them to misery!

The Buddha said, "Mistaking the false for the true and the true for the false, you overlook the heart." The right view is the heart view. The heart view is what's really going on at the heart of the matter aside from any concepts.

There would be no existential angst if they were just a little upset that they had to do taxes instead of going to the beach on a nice day. That's the heart of the matter. However, a tremendous amount of anguish arises when what's really going on, the truth, is different from our conceptual modeling, the way we think things should be.

This is why people get so upset on Christmas. The holiday season is filled with depression in America. Why is this? Because people's actual experiences do not measure up to their model's flawed view. Our society paints a rather rosy model of how Christmas should be. So on Christmas Day, kids end up unhappy because they didn't get the toys they wanted and saw on TV. Adults get depressed on Christmas because their families are not together or they don't feel jolly and wonderful like they think they should during the holidays.

Assignment: Photo Identification

Get an old picture of yourself. Find a picture of yourself when you were young, say a toddler, or a preteen.

If you can't find an old picture of yourself, write the description of yourself and your world when you were five. Describe how you looked, where you lived, what you did, who your friends were, everything.

Now look at that picture or the description and write on a new page in your Enlightenment Journal entitled "Photo Identification" either "Yes" or "No" to answer this question:

Is that you?

Complete this assignment now. Continue reading when finished.

Post Assignment

From the assignment you can expose your model of life. According to your model, the person in the picture is you, but according to reality, it is ridiculous to think that it is you. You are much taller! What you know and are aware of is vastly greater than the person in the picture. That person does not exist anymore. You exist now. The only thing that ties you to the belief that the person in the pictures is you is your model, your frozen view of reality.

When asked by the Emperor of China, "Who are you, what is your spiritual lineage, and what is your attainment?" Bodhidharma, an Enlightened teacher and the founder of Zen Buddhism, answered, "I am no one, of no lineage, and I know nothing."

A fluid view of the world would be to view yourself as no one in particular. A fluid view of self reveals that in every moment you are a new person. In every moment your boyfriend, coworker, and mother are new people. In every moment everything that appears in your life is new. In every moment life is new.

As your awareness expands, who you are changes. When you were ten years old, your state of mind and description of the world then were true for you. Now you can see that at ten years old the truth you were aware of was very limited. As you grew older and learned more, your awareness of life grew and your description of the world changed. This offered you more opportunities and complexities in life and changed you into a different person. Now your current state of mind and description of the world is true for you.

With the teachings of Enlightenment you can continue to expand your awareness and change into a completely new person! Every moment that you become more aware of life you change into a new person. With a greater awareness of life you become a new person in a brighter state of being. You become a person who has more options for happiness. You become a person who can handle difficulties with greater perspective. You become more Enlightened.

Assignment: Who Am I Really?

Having exposed your conceptual model for viewing the world with all its definitions and stories, now write down who you really are.

In an earlier assignment entitled "The Stories of My Life," you described a partial view of yourself. You described your life based on your occupation, your personal strengths, what had happened to you, your relationships, and what you think about life. Is that all that you are?

Abandon any mental models, views of the world, or descriptions of the past. Who are you beyond all the roles that you have played in life? Who are you beyond your relationships? Who are you beyond who you've always thought you were? Who are you beyond your past?

Please open your Enlightenment Journal to a new page and entitle it, "Who Am I Really?" Enter your reflections of your right view of yourself.

Complete this assignment now. Continue reading when finished.

Right Intent

Right intent is the secret to success in any endeavor in life. Before words and actions, even before thoughts and feelings, comes intention. With the right intent, you will have the right thoughts and feelings, which will lead to the right words and actions to succeed in anything, even Enlightenment. When you lack right intent, no matter what you do, it will detract from your happiness and Enlightenment.

Once a group of monks were preparing to go out and feed some nearby lepers. Their teacher, seeing them getting ready to depart, asked them, "What do you intend to do?"

The monks answered, "We are going to feed the lepers to aid our Enlightenment by getting the good karma that comes from a selfless act."

The teacher said, "Then you're just wasting your time."

Intention is your power of choice. If you are reading this now, you have intended and chosen to learn the teachings of Enlightenment. You use intention to choose more evolving thoughts and activities. You use intention to uproot desires and to face fears. Before there is any manifestation of karma, we have the power of intention.

If you use the power of intent selfishly you can gain many things! You can gain money, you can gain position, and you can gain every type of transient experience. You can gain anything and everything you desire, but it won't last. Selfish intent is transient. What you gain from it, you will inevitably lose. It is only with right intent, selfless intent, that you gain love, Enlightenment, and an awareness of that which is eternal.

Once a man posed a question to his Buddhist teacher, "The world is so confusing, who's to say what good intention is? Some say that the road to evil is paved with good intentions. Some say that the Nazis, though they did bad things, had good intentions. Couldn't one person's good intentions be confused and actually cause harm?"

His teacher answered, "Yes, both good and bad intentions exist in duality. Both good and bad intentions are selfish intentions. Both good and bad intentions lead to suffering. In duality one person's good may be considered evil by another. Yet right intention is always intention that is congruent with life. Right intention exists beyond duality. Right intention is truth itself."

To talk about knowing what right intention is, I recall a passage from *The Little Prince*: "It is only with the heart that one sees rightly. What is essential is invisible to the eye."

Right intention is simple. Right intention is intention that brings love, happiness, and awakening. Right intention comes from the heart. All of us know in our hearts what is right intent and wrong intent. If someone is acting out of wrong intent, they may be able to reason and explain their good intentions, but it never matches the truth you know in your heart.

People are like onions. They have many layers of intent in every activity and in every relationship. Most people are only aware of their surface intentions, but deep down inside there's a lot more going on.

Many people harbor negative layers of intent beneath a positive surface. Primarily unaware of their bad intentions, they sabotage the things and relationships that could make them happy. It requires mature self-reflection and honesty to know yourself and your intent. Most people leave their uncomfortable and dark feelings unattended.

Realization is liberation. When you realize selfish and dark intent is there, it vanishes in the light of your discrimination. For the Enlightened all layers of intent are unified. The Enlightened only intend Enlightenment. They only intend awakening. They only intend awareness. Enlightened intent is the movement of life.

Assignment: My Intent

Entitle a new page in your Enlightenment Journal, "My Intent." Write down your intent in accomplishing your existing goals. Write down your intent toward the people in your life. After you've listed your intentions, you will examine your intent closely. You will account for all of your layers.

For each intention you listed, ask yourself "Why?" over and over. Ask yourself "Why?" about each line of intent till there are no more "Why's" to ask. When you know all the answers to the relevant "Why's" for a subject, only then will you know your intent. For example:

Intention – I want to get a promotion at work!
Why?
So I will have more money.
Why?
So I can buy a new sports car.
Why?
So I can show everyone how cool I am.
Why?
So that girls like me.
Why?
So I can get a girlfriend.

Intention – I want to help Suzie become a cheerleader.
Why?
So that she can get on the squad.
Why?
So that I can hang out with her more.
Why?
So that I can meet her brother who I think is cute.

Be honest. In the light of your reflection on intent you can purify your intent towards all things in your life. Understand what your intent is for all of the important things in your life and measure your intent by your heart.

Complete this assignment now. Continue reading when finished.

Assignment: Intention

Entitle a new page in your Enlightenment Journal, "Intention."

Write down the story of a time when you had good intent. Write down the story of another time when you had bad intent.

Describe the difference in how each story made you feel, no matter what the outcome was.

Complete this assignment now. Continue reading when finished.

Right Speech

Right speech is speaking in terms of the other person's interests. It is speaking of truth in a way that is accessible to the listener's conceptual model. Right speech opens opportunities. It never closes the doors of possibility. Right speech relieves oppression. It never pushes others down. Right speech empowers. It never controls.

Right speech is primarily listening. If you speak first without listening, your speech is often selfish and not useful to the listener. If you listen first, then your speech will be addressing the condition and situation of the listener.

It is also very important to listen without coming to negative conclusions. Even if the teller of a story believes that the situation is bad and describes conditions of great concern and suffering, there are still endless opportunities for awakening and evolution. Concluding negativity from another's speech closes the door on opportunities for awakening.

When someone tells me of the complications of their troubles and difficulties, I always say to them, "You know what I don't see here? A problem!" Then I help them to see solutions. Speaking of solutions is right speech.

Do not speak of problems; speak of solutions. When you hear of problems, listen with the intention of finding solutions.

Judgments say a lot more about the one casting the judgment than the one being judged. So if Jessica comes to you and says, "Debbie is so mean! She said you were fugly," then what do you know about Debbie? Not much. However, you would know a lot about Jessica.

You cannot ascertain the truth of Debbie's words or intentions from what Jessica tells you. Even if you love and trust Jessica, she could be mistaken, confused, or have selfish motives. What you can tell from Jessica's judgment is that Jessica's ego is riled up and that she is spreading discord.

Listening to negative speech about another person poisons your mind. Speaking in judgment or ill will of another strengthens the limitations of your own attention.

Judgments reveal imperfections in your own outlook and attention. If you cast judgments on others, you expose the very thing you judge to be your own imperfection. If you judge, you allow that imperfection to exist in your own mind. Judgments draw your mind from the peace of unity to the sorrows of transient duality.

Do not judge others. Rather, consider the imperfections that you see in others as the imperfections of your own outlook. When you listen to the judgments of others, do not be poisoned with the limitations of their outlook. Rather, accept the information just as it is, as their judgment.

If a friend tells you that he saw a new film that you have tickets to see and that it's a terrible film that you'll hate, if you take his judgment as truth, when you see the film you'll look for what he said is terrible and what he said you will hate. Because you believed his judgment to be true, your experience will be tainted by his negative outlook. On the other hand, if you take the judgment as just his judgment, then you'll just know that your friend really didn't like the film and be able to experience the film yourself without any negative filters or modifications.

Buddha said of right speech, "The Enlightened speak the truth, are devoted to the truth, and are reliable and worthy of confidence. They never knowingly deceive others for the sake of their own advantage. What they have heard here they do not repeat there, so as to cause dissension there. Thus, they unite those who are divided and those that are united they encourage. Concord gladdens them. They delight and rejoice in concord, and it is concord that they spread by their words. They avoid harsh language and speak such words as are gentle and soothing to the ear, loving, going to the heart, courteous and dear, and agreeable to many. They avoid vain talk and speak at the right time in accordance with facts, speak what is useful, speak about right wisdom and right practice. Their speech is like treasure at the right moment, accompanied by arguments moderate and full of sense."

Right speech includes lying. Now lying, the way most people see it, means speech that is in conflict with truth. When commonly, selfishly, and ignorantly applied, lying ruins your peace of mind and is not conducive to awakening.

However, there are times where lying is not lying. That is to say that there are times when lying is not in conflict with a larger truth. Consider that speech is merely syntax. There are times when the incorrect syntax you use does not put your attention in opposition to truth. There are times that require incorrect syntax in order to serve truth.

"Thou shall not lie!" is a frozen concept. What if Darth Vader is asking you where the secret rebel base is located so that he can fly over in the Death Star and blow up your planet? If you told him the truth, would that be right speech? Thou wouldst not have lied, but thou wouldst have spoken wrongly. Always speak in a way that serves life. That is right speech.

There once was a gal who read a book about right speech. Misinterpreting the Buddha's teachings she decided that 100% honesty was the best policy. One day, she was having lunch with two friends. Just as they started eating, she said,

"Todd, I'm just saying this to be honest with you, but I don't like it when you wear that leather jacket because it always reminds me that you support the killing of poor defenseless animals."

Taking off his jacket and putting it to the side, Todd said, "Oh, you don't like my jacket? I don't support the killing of poor defenseless animals! It's just that my dad gave me this jacket for my birthday."

They all sat quietly eating until again she broke the silence addressing her other friend, "Lorraine, I'm just saying this to be honest with you, but you eating that hamburger after what I just said to Todd really upsets me. Plus, maybe laying off the hamburgers would help you with that weight problem that you're always complaining about!"

Lorraine put down her hamburger, and after a moment burst into tears. Shocked by Lorraine's response, she said, "What? I'm just being honest!"

Right speech isn't always saying what you think is right all the time. Even if what you have to say serves life, you have to say it at the proper time, in the proper way, so that it will bring peace, harmony, and awakening. It is better to say nothing than to say something that will cause harm.

I recall the story told by a woman who was a child leader during the Chinese Cultural Revolution. At a very young age she was conditioned to believe that Chairman Mao was a god, that communism was the path to truth, and that exposing enemies of the state was the greatest good that one could do.

On one occasion, she received an order from an official of the state to declare her middle school teacher to be an enemy of the state. At a large assembly she stood before her teacher, fellow students, state officials, and police and declared her teacher to be an enemy. She knew this would ruin the teacher's life, but she did it because she thought it was her duty and responsibility.

The teacher denied the accusation and announced that someone must have put the young girl up to it. The teacher stood before the young girl and asked her to look her in the eyes and tell everyone if in her heart she really believed this allegation was true. She looked into her teacher's eyes and saw a person who had taught her, empowered her, who had disciplined her when she was bad and cared for her when she was sick. She looked into the eyes that had only ever showed her truth, possibility, and love.

Although she was conditioned to believe that the greatest good for her country and god was to say that the allegation was true, she stood there with tears running down her cheeks unable to speak. When speaking from the heart she had no words to say against her teacher. That is right speech.

You can't affix commandments or rules to speech. Rules are meant to be broken. You can only be fluid and speak what is right, now. Speak of what is Enlightening. Speak of what will aid awakening.

Assignment: Speaking of the Day

Spend a day observing your speech and written communications. What is your intent in saying the things you do?

Also when you hear people make judgments of others, what do you know from their judgments? When you hear people speak of problems, are you concluding limitation or are you seeing possibilities? What truth do your words serve? Write an Enlightenment Journal entry entitled, "Speaking of the Day."

Complete this assignment now. Continue reading when finished.

Right Action

Right action is perfect action. Right action is action that is in accordance with truth. Right action is pure action. It is complete action. It is action that is unhindered. It is free action.

Fears and doubts hinder our actions. We doubt we can do something or are afraid of failing.

One afternoon, a 12 year-old boy rode the subway home from a friend's house. The subway car was quite full. All of the seats were taken and men and women stood throughout the car.

All of a sudden there was a commotion at one end of the car. A pickpocket amongst a group of six young adult hoodlums had been caught by a woman as he reached into her purse. She shrieked and pulled away from him. He grabbed the whole of her purse and started pulling. She, holding her purse strap, would not give up. They were in a tug of war. The other hoodlums stood watchful of others around in the subway car. All the men and women standing at that end of the car cleared away from the struggle, cramming backward toward the center of the car.

The struggle continued, with him yanking her purse and her pulling it back. The boy looked for a moment to the men and women who retreated into the huddled mass. They all had a look of shock and concern, but steadily stepped backward and away from the struggle. The pickpocket swung to the right clutching the purse. This uprooted the woman and she fell to the ground, but still clung to the purse strap.

Now an elderly Chinese woman sitting across from where the woman fell planted her walking stick firmly to her left and pulled herself to a standing position with her right hand grasping her chair's safety bar. In heavily accented English the grey haired woman said, "Leave her alone! You leave her alone now!"

The pickpocket and the rest of the hoodlums looked at the little Chinese woman standing across from them. The pickpocket tried to yank the purse free one more time to no avail then ran to the exit door. The rest of the hoodlums followed suit. They fled into the adjacent car and exited the train at the next station.

The woman secured her purse and stood up straightening her jacket. She took the right hand of the Chinese woman in between both of her hands in a warm shake and said with a smile of gratitude, "You are my hero, thank you." The elderly Chinese woman smiled, nodded her head and then sat back down in her seat.

The woman who'd been assaulted then turned to the men and women who had begun to uncluster from their retreat. She looked at them with piercing eyes and yelled, "You cowards!" Everyone was silent and bowed their heads in shame.

Everyone who stepped away, or just stayed seated knew that they too could have done something to help. They could have done the right thing. They could have taken right action, but they didn't because of fear and doubt.

The young boy was afraid too, but he learned something. Inspired by the nobility of the elderly Chinese woman's courage to take right action, he learned a lesson for life. He learned a lesson of right action. He was only 12 years old at the time, but imagined himself being the hero, directing the wrongdoers away.

Four years later, as he was walking home from a music lesson, he saw two men holding a knife up to the neck of an elderly woman in an alley. She clinched her purse handle in fear, though they threatened her life. The young man remembering the power of right action stepped into the alley and shouted, "Leave her alone! You leave her alone now!" The two men, startled, halted their assault and ran away, leaving their victim in peace.

On another occasion, a man had a heart attack while dining at a fine dinning restaurant. As the man fell to the ground, his wife screamed for help at his side. Forty onlookers, waiters and customers, stood by while the man died.

It turns out that 18 of the onlookers had taken a CPR course at some time in their lives, and that another 4 of the onlookers held valid CPR training certifications. Of the 40 onlookers, 22 could have done something to help save a life. They could've tried, but they didn't.

In reviewing the incident report, the Red Cross contacted these 22 people and asked them why they didn't try to help. They all said that they experienced fear, and in the face of fear, didn't really comprehend the gravity of what was going on. They all said that they thought about helping, then immediately doubted their skills and their ability to help. Later, upon reflection, all of them said that they knew they should have tried.

It's not hard to see what right action is when you think about it, or reflect upon it, but right action doesn't take place in the past. Right action is right now. Are you awake? Do you have the presence of mind to stop injustice, or save a life, right now? Fear stops you from seeing what's happening and from knowing that you have the power to do something about it.

Assignment: Fear Factor

Entitle a new page in your Enlightenment Journal, "Fear Factor."

Consider events and experiences in your life. Describe a time where you did not take right action because of fear or doubt. It may have been something habitual, like being unable to say "No" to a person because you were afraid that they wouldn't like you. Or perhaps it was something disempowering, like being afraid to take initiative at work. In reflecting on this, consider why you were afraid or doubtful. Describe your fears and doubts in detail.

Next, describe a time where you did take right action. Did you face any fear? Did you have to overcome any doubt? Describe your fears and doubts in detail.

Complete this assignment now. Continue reading when finished.

Passions, Should-Do's, and Right Action

Often desires and ideas of what we should do hinder our actions. Our passions compel us into impure action. Our concepts of what we "should do" confuse us and hide from us the right action to take.

We fill our minds with petty things because we fancy the thought that if we have more to choose from, we will be able to choose the perfect thing. However, with so many desires and concepts, it's hard for us to know what's right.

Once a young man asked a Buddhist teacher about some difficulties he was having in his life. He said, "I'm trying to do so many things at the same time that nothing is working out. How do you know what the right thing for you to do is?"

"It's simple," the teacher said. "Follow your true smile!"

"How do I do that?" the young man asked.

The teacher said, "Tell me your situation, and we'll find your true smile together."

The young man agreed and started speaking quickly with a frowning brow, "I want to move to Los Angeles to become a movie star! But I come from a proper family and they would not support that. My father is a lawyer, as is my grandfather. My older brother is studying to pass the bar now. So instead of being a movie star, I'm supposed to be a lawyer, even though right now I'm in pre-med. Oh, and Peggy, my girlfriend for ten years wants to get married."

The teacher nodded and said, "I can see why it's so difficult for you."

"Tell me," the young man said, "What is it?"

The teacher answered, "The trouble is that you put too many things into one thing. It's much simpler than that. Let's break it down together."

The young man nodded with a bit of a confused look on his face. The teacher asked him, "Do you think it's right that you go to LA to become a movie star?" The young man smiled as if he had received a present on Christmas Day, then a moment later shook his head as if discovering that his present was a pair of tube socks. "Nah, it doesn't actually seem right. It's just a fantasy I guess, like when I was eleven and wanted to run away to join the circus. But I know now that desire wasn't really right. Plus, there are so many talented actors in LA that for me to be successful would honestly be a one in a million chance."

"So then," the teacher asked, "Do you truly want to become a lawyer?"

The young man shook his head with a sour look as if he had tasted something unsavory and said, "Even though I always thought I would be a lawyer, now I think it's just not for me."

"Well then," the teacher said, "You mentioned you were in pre-med now, what about becoming a doctor?"

The young man pondered becoming a doctor and said, "Learning medicine is fun! Actually it's fascinating to me. And doctors are respectable in good society!"

"Ah-ha!" the teacher shouted as he pointed at the young man's face. "That's your true smile!"

The young man noticed that in considering becoming a doctor, his concerns and interests in becoming a movie star and lawyer fell away. He found that a comfortably genuine smile had formed on his face. Filled with joy in finding the right action, the young man exclaimed with a bright laugh, "Just follow your true smile! How brilliant!"

The teacher nodded and immediately asked, "Now how about marrying Peggy?" The young man's smile vanished as his jaw dropped and brow furrowed. The teacher burst into laughter. The young man, realizing his facial expression, nodded knowingly and burst into laughter as well.

Assignment: Smiles

Of the things you're doing in life, what makes you smile? Of the choices you have to make, which make you smile?

Entitle a new page in your Enlightenment Journal, "Smiles!"

Write down the primary activities, relationships, and choices in your life. Consider them each carefully one at a time. Use a mirror to observe your facial expressions after considering each. Draw your facial expression next to each.

Complete this assignment now. Continue reading when finished.

Society's Dream and Right Action

Often, social conditioning and peer pressures dictate or hinder our actions. We act in the mentality of our herd, doing things because everyone else does and because people expect us to.

A woman once approached a Buddhist teacher at a public meditation seminar and asked, "Have I done the right thing with my life?"

She further explained, "While I was growing up I was always told that the right thing for me to do was to eat kosher, marry a good Jewish boy, and make babies. Now I'm fat, have been married for ten years, and have two children."

She continued, "My husband and children are great, but sometimes I wonder why I have them. Now I think that if I could do it all over again, I would invest more energy in pursuing my own happiness.

"The only reason that I got married is because everyone was telling me that I needed to get married before it was too late. Even when I was 17 my aunts would say, 'When I was your age, I was already engaged. It would be a pity if you missed your chance to find a good Jewish boy!' So I did everything that everyone told me I should do. I was a good Jewish girl and became a good Jewish wife and mother. Even though I did what they told me would make me happy, the truth is that I knew I wasn't happy. I was just kept busy and my mind occupied.

"I've done everything I was told I should do in life, but I feel like I haven't done anything that I want to do with my life. At this point, I don't even know what I can do with my life. I'm older and have less energy. I feel like I gave my life away to everyone else and now I have nothing left. So I have come to ask you, have I done the right thing with my life?"

The teacher responded, "You can judge your past experiences if you want, but I will tell you that in your life, now, in this moment, you can do the right thing. The past is no longer here, but your awareness is! So right now, you can do things that evolve you. You can do things that are empowering and Enlightening right now! No one has wasted their life when they seek evolution in this moment."

The teacher continued, "This is how it works on the pathway to Enlightenment. You learn that your initial dreams and concepts are limited. Then you learn that life is bigger than what you knew. Then you keep learning that life offers endless opportunities for fulfillment. This moment is your life. Don't waste now."

I met a retired American woman in a remote Buddhist monastery in Thailand. She told me that she had not heard of Buddhism for the first 62 years of her life. One year before her husband's death they visited Asia on vacation. While in Thailand, her husband urged her to visit a Buddhist temple with him and take a class on Buddhism that the monks offered in English. She, considering herself to be a good Christian, was initially opposed to this idea, but then acquiesced on a whim of curiosity.

In attending the class they discovered to their surprise that they loved the Buddhist teachings! They were both deeply transformed from their experiences during the class. She and her husband couldn't imagine that Eastern spirituality could be so relevant to them. They identified with the truth of the teachings and were moved by the poignant beauty of the Buddhist way. On that day, they both took the vows of a lay practitioner and became Buddhists.

After her husband's death she took up residence at the monastery. Her view of possibilities had been transformed and she was open to the adventure. She said, "I don't regret not learning of the Buddhist path for the first 62 years of my life because I'm traveling on it now!"

Assignment: Herd Views

Entitle a page in your Enlightenment Journal, "Herd Views."

What are the social conditions that affect your life, choices, and actions? What are the expectations and peer pressures put on you by others? Write about the social conditions and pressures that affect you.

Write about what actions you could take to overcome the conditions and pressures that you face now. What actions could lead you to a greater awareness and a greater possibility of happiness and truth?

Complete this assignment now. Continue reading when finished.

Right Action in Motion

In its time, a wave will grow in the sea and crash on the beach. The wave's welling up, cresting, and crashing are a perfect movement. This is right action.

We can experience right action when we engage in movement with perfect form. The perfection of motion comes when we become the motion. When the dancer lets go of ideas of what's good and bad in dancing, he has become free to move perfectly. When the dancer lets go of ambition and inhibition, his dance becomes a sacred expression of truth. When the dancer loses any notion of himself and just dances, this is right action. This is when the dancer becomes the dance. Now there is no dancer. There is only the movement of life.

A lot of athletes experience perfect motion from time to time. They call it "The Zone." The Zone is when you're down by two points and intercept a lay-up in front of your basket. You look at the time clock and there's three seconds, two seconds, you're not yet to mid-court. An opposing guard is just reaching you, now's the time, you take the shot! The ball sails just to the left of the defending guard's hand. As the ball flies through the air, the buzzer rings. You watch as the ball nears its target, and then, "Swoosh!" You score a three-pointer!

After leading the Chicago Bulls to a narrow NBA championship victory by scoring the winning point in a long shot, far from the basket at the last possible moment of the game, Michael Jordan was asked, "What happened during those last moments of the game?"

Jordan responded, "I was completely in the moment. I was totally focused. The basket's rim was amazingly clear in my vision. On the last shot to win the game, just as the buzzer sounded, I just elevated and shot the ball....Swoosh!"

Athletes love The Zone. That's when they feel most alive. The Zone has no thoughts. The Zone is pure motion and perfect form. A tad too slow or an inch to the left, and you'd have no goal. With right action success is certain.

In martial arts, right action is an imperative practice. The samurai would call it "being the sword." The perfect action of the sword is to kill. The perfect action of the samurai was to let go of their human mind and be one with the perfect action of the sword.

Assignment: Being the Dance

Dance. Become the dance. Dance to your favorite and most danceable music! See if you can disappear in the motion.

If you don't like dance or can't dance very well this assignment is even better for you! My Buddhist teacher said that learning to dance was one of the best things he ever did in life! Dancing is wonderful. If you don't like dance or have difficulty dancing well, it's because you let your thoughts block your experience.

People have so many concepts built up around dance. They think that they can do it or that they can't. They build up algorithms into their views that introduce sexuality and "being cool" into dance. They create layer upon layer of ideas that are integrated into their conceptual models describing what dance is.

Dance is just dance. Just dancing is magical. Just dancing is right action. Give it a shot. Dance for a few minutes. Relax and let go! Express yourself in motion. Dance is exhilarating! Move your body and be free of what limits you!

Dance alone, so that you won't be disturbed by others. Dance in the dark or in a dimly lit area. Darkness helps you let go of the physical focus. Dance to the best, most fun music that makes you feel good. Feel the music. Move to the music. Yield the self and thoughts to become the motion.

Write about your experience in your Enlightenment Journal. Open a new page in your Enlightenment Journal and entitle it, "Being the Dance."

Complete this assignment now. Continue reading when finished.

Right Job

A right job or livelihood is a job that is conducive to your awakening. This doesn't mean that you have to become a welfare worker, a nun, or a volunteer for some good cause. Rather, it means that you should make money doing something that evolves you and makes you happy.

Making money is good. A lot of spiritual people have an aversion to money because they see people with money doing bad things. The money itself is not bad. What is bad are some of the things people do with money. These same people often do bad things with love as well, but we don't think love is bad just because we see others making mistakes with it.

Money is a kind of power. You can use the power for good or you can use the power for evil. It is up to you. With great power comes great responsibility. Without attention to the responsibilities of handling power properly, power can cause harm. With common care and the lack of greed, money is very positive.

In the same way, consider fire as a power. Fire can be used as a weapon. Fire has the power to keep you warm when the cold temperature would make you ill. Fire has the power to light your path so that you don't fall and hurt yourself in the dark. Without attention to the responsibilities of handling fire properly, fire can cause tremendous unintended harm.

A lot of spiritual people think it is simpler to be poor and not focus on making money. However, they often struggle in draining jobs and worry about paying their bills. Spending eight to ten hours of your day in a draining job and worrying about paying your bills does not add to your awakening. Instead these weigh down on your mind like a ton of bricks.

Have you ever been in serious debt or known someone in serious debt who has gotten out of that debt? A student of mine took three years to get out of $25,000 of debt. When she was out of debt, she said that it felt as if she had removed an 800-pound gorilla from her back!

Debt and financial worry severely drain your spiritual power. It is important to find balance in your financial life. You must make enough money to afford a dwelling that is conducive to awakening. You must make enough money to afford the food, clothing, transportation, and the other things that you need to support your practice.

Also, if you have even more money than you need, you can help others in ways that are conducive to truth and awakening. If you make as much money as you can and are in a strong financial position, you can insulate yourself from the heavy energies of the world and help others. This way you can create positive structures for spiritual practice that benefit many.

Buddha includes work as part of the spiritual path to Enlightenment because it is part of the spiritual path to Enlightenment! It is good to focus on work. Some spiritual people consider their day job to be separate from their spiritual path. Buddha suggests that your day job should be an integral part of your spiritual path.

What is a proper job to have that makes money and is conducive to awakening? The evils of the world seem so entangled in any industry and any job. If you work in apparel, you may find that the clothing you sell has been made by child labor in sweatshops on the Malaysian border. If you work in produce, you may find that the workers who harvest the vegetables you sell are Guatemalan refugees who make $1.15 an hour and live in cardboard shacks. How can you do any job in this country, when your income tax supports a military that kills people? How is this conducive to Enlightenment?

A student once asked his Buddhist teacher, "Should I find a new job? I have been working on the staff of a state politician for three years. I believe in this politician. I believe that he's really trying to help people and that his policies are the best way to do it."

He paused with an unsure look on his face and continued, "A couple weeks ago, I was having lunch with a friend who's on the staff of an opposing politician. My friend told me his ideas about policy and they seem good though different than mine. Then he told me why he believed some of my politician's policies were bad. He drew a dark, bleak picture of the policies I believe in. He quoted convincing data from reputable sources. I never thought about the policies that I support in that light. He made it seem that the policies I support were going to bring ruin to the state and that the politician I serve is the greatest evil of our time."

His teacher asked him, "I understand your problem, but new data aside, how has your job been in the past couple of weeks?"

He thought for a moment, and then said, "Well it's been great! Actually, I've just been appointed to be the head of a new coalition to organize all of the state's congressmen on a bill to save the open spaces in the marsh and forest. I'm really excited about this campaign because it's something that matters to me."

His teacher shook his head, "There's no need for you to find a new job. You are having a good time in an empowering position. This is a right job!" The student nodded with a bit of relief and said, "But what if it turns out that my politician is dumping toxic waste or something?"

His teacher said, "Any way that you make a living may lead to profit someone who does evil. Another's evil doing is his or her own responsibility. Trust your feelings. If your work is fun and rewarding to you then there is something right about it for you. On the other hand, even if you work for the most benign company in the world, if you don't feel so happy at your job, then it will be time to get a new job.

"If your politician does bad things, eventually you would feel it in your work. You would see harmful policies, negative actions, and abusive management. These kinds of negative conditions would upset the positive feelings you have about your work. This is when you would clearly know that it is time to find another job."

If you do not have great mastery and investment in a particular career path, computer science is a great field. Computer science is an excellent livelihood for spiritual seekers. People who are drawn to meditation excel in computer science as a profession. In computer science you exercise and strengthen your mind. In computer science you practice formulations of structured, relational, and hierarchical logic. Many advanced spiritual practices require similar disciplines.

Computer programming is an exciting field. Computer programming is like solving puzzles. From creating innovative web technologies to automating banking systems to developing mobile phone applications, there are unlimited technical pursuits to explore. Computer science is also an evolving field. As a computer programmer you are always practicing beginner's mind. You are always learning new things, new technologies, and new ways of using your mind.

Computer science is also a very respected profession with good working conditions. As a computer programmer you can work in virtually any company, in any industry, anywhere in the world. Computer science also pays the highest rates in professional wage scales. As a computer programmer you can earn large sums of money to support yourself, your practice, and others.

While at for a dot-com in San Francisco, I met another programmer who was a Buddhist monk and had spent his last 20 years living in a monastery in India. I asked him why he had left the monastery to become a computer programmer. "Right job is my next spiritual lesson," he answered.

Assignment: Right Job Evaluation

Entitle a new Enlightenment Journal page, "Right Job Evaluation."

Consider what you do for a living or what you plan on doing for a living. Write your observations for the following considerations:

1. Is it conducive to Enlightenment?
2. How does it evolve you?
3. What do you get out of your work?

Complete this assignment now. Continue reading when finished.

Assignment: Job Evolution

Now, just for the sake of exploration, what are your other career options? Entitle a new Enlightenment Journal page, "Job Evolution."

List all of your career options, all alternative careers that are feasible for you. Include computer science as a career option in this assignment.

For each career option, answer the same three questions as for the evaluation of your current job:

1. Is it conducive to Enlightenment?
2. How does it evolve you?
3. What do you get out of your work?

Complete this assignment now. Continue reading when finished.

Right Effort

When we hear the word "effort," we are ready for hard work. Doing anything takes effort. When we want to achieve something great or get something valuable, we think it will require arduous effort. However, right effort is easy. Right effort is natural.

Upon being honored with a prestigious award by his company, a software architect who had successfully designed a complex Artificial Intelligence system for identifying fraudulent insurance claims smiled with great satisfaction as he received a commemoratively inscribed crystal plaque. In a speech to the executives he said, "It took ten months of demanding labor, strenuous attention, and many all-nighters, but it was easy because I loved every minute of it!"

Loving is right effort! When you love what you do, effort is easy. Love itself is a powerful force. When you are aligned with love, right effort is effortless.

When there is something that we don't want to do, every bit of effort is arduous work. Many people in the working world do their work as if they were a child whose mother had just told them, "Clean your room and do your homework or there'll be no TV for you tonight!" If you don't love your job, then the effort it takes to do your work is exhausting.

When there is something that we want to do, even though there are many activities involved and a lot of hard work to do, the effort is easy, happy, and empowering. The effort seems to just flow from us. Right effort is aligning ourselves with that natural flow.

A Buddhist master described right effort when after finishing a 12 hour meditation session, a young monk asked him, "Master, isn't it hard to meditate for so long?"

The Buddhist master replied, "Enlightenment is the easiest thing in the universe!"

There was once an excited new Zen student who asked his new teacher, "If I meditate really hard and am dedicated to my studies, how long will it take to attain Enlightenment?" The Zen master looked carefully at his student and said, "20 years."

The Zen student shook his head and said, "No, you don't understand. I mean, I will meditate really really hard. I'm a very accomplished student. I've always been at the top of my class. I will pick up all the teachings quickly and do everything you say. So, now what do you think?"

The Zen master looked carefully at his student and said, "I misjudged, 30 years."

The Zen student looked shocked and said, "But I..."

The Zen master cut him off, saying, "40 years."

You don't go about Enlightenment the same way you go about other things. One step forward in ego effort is two steps backward in right effort.

A student who had recently started studying with a Buddhist teacher had previously been training in martial arts for ten years. The Buddhist teacher, who was also a martial arts teacher, asked the young man if he'd like to learn something about Enlightenment through the practice of martial arts. "Yes!" The young man nodded with great interest. The Buddhist master invited the young man to attend his martial arts classes in the evenings. Very confident in his martial arts skills, the young man accepted.

The Buddhist teacher's system of martial arts was new for the young man, so like all new students, he wore a white belt in the class. The beginning lessons were basic stances, blocking, and striking forms. After a couple of months, the Buddhist teacher had the white belts do some sparring matches. The young man considered himself to be excellent in sparring and had a lot of experience sparring in his previous martial arts practice. He was excited about beginning the sparring practice in his Buddhist teacher's class and was sure he'd do well in the matches.

To his shock and dismay, all of the white belts beat him on his first day of sparring. He was stifled in his technique. His own speed tripped him up. His attempts at defense seemed to only set him up for an attack. Guys and gals who were completely new to martial arts were scoring points on him and defeating him in sparring matches.

The next day, he approached his Buddhist teacher and asked, "What's wrong with me? I'm doing horribly! I am so frustrated! All of my best attacks and strongest defenses do not work against white belts! It's as if I don't know anything about martial arts at all!"

His teacher smiled and said, "Then don't know anything at all! Stop trying the way you know and start trying the way you don't know. Your self effort won't work. This system of martial arts is a Buddhist practice, a spiritual consideration of selflessness. Selfless effort is required."

In the next class the young man stopped trying the way he knew and selflessly followed the teachings of the class. In time something unexpected happened: he had a lot of fun and found that he learned a lot more about martial arts. On the day that he passed his black belt test, his Buddhist teacher said, "Now you have learned right action."

Just as Yoda described in some of his last words to Luke, "A Jedi's power flows from the force." Similarly to Luke, the young man learned that from the force of right effort, a powerful and spiritual dimension of martial arts is revealed.

The habitual way that people use effort for accomplishing tasks is the toilsome way of an obsessed mind. We always think, "I am going to get something out of this for my effort." We are obsessed with self gaining in every endeavor. Yet for all of our trying, obsessed effort never brings us the results we crave. In our desperate efforts to gain, we are never truly satisfied.

Right effort expects no outcome or profit. Right effort is a force not for gaining, but a force for balancing. Right effort is never obsessed. Right effort is free and brings satisfaction.

Once, a lay practitioner of Tantra was visiting his teacher at the monastery late in the evening. He told his teacher that he was very inspired by all that he had learned. He said that now he really wanted to try to know truth. He told his teacher that he was considering studying some of the advanced doctrines to learn the most precious spiritual truths.

He asked his teacher, "How can I best try to know truth?"

His teacher picked up an ancient Indian text. This scroll contained some of the most advanced doctrines of their lineage. Holding the scroll, his teacher walked to the left of the lay practitioner and through an open sliding door. He now stood outside on the deck several feet away from where they sat together.

The lay practitioner stayed seated with a great deal of enthusiasm. He knew that with the special scroll, his attempts at attaining truth would be certain!

Reaching the edge of the deck, the teacher dropped the scroll. The scroll fell into the darkness of the night and rustled the shrubbery below. The lay practitioner leaped to his feet in surprise!

His teacher went down on his hands and knees. He started searching the deck floor in the light cast from a nearby wall lantern. The lay practitioner hurried over and peered into the darkness where the scroll had fallen. He was unable to see anything in the pitch black night.

He then looked back to his teacher who was carefully investigating the deck far from where the scroll had fallen. Though it made no sense to him, he then went down on his hands and knees as well and started looking at the deck floor.

After a few minutes of searching the barren floor, the lay practitioner asked his teacher, "Why are we looking here? The scroll fell over the deck into the shrubbery."

His teacher replied, "We're looking here because there is no light over there!" The lay practitioner responded, "But even though it's dark there, the scroll is also there!"

"Yes, the scroll is there," the teacher retorted, "But if you spend your time looking in the dark, you'll exhaust yourself with your efforts. At best all you may gain is a scroll and some words, both of which are useless in the dark! On the other hand if you put your effort into looking where there is light you will always find what you're looking for: truth."

The lay practitioner realized what his teacher was showing him. He sat with his teacher and gazed at the floor in wonder. He then entered Samadhi and knew truth.

Assignment: Effortless

Create a new Enlightenment Journal entry. Entitle the page, "Effortless."

Consider events and experiences in the past. Write an account of a time when you didn't have much fun in accomplishing a task. What were your efforts like?

Write an account of a time when you had a lot of fun accomplishing a task. What were your efforts like?

You'll see that the amount of work, attention, difficulty, and effort is not what makes something fun or not, but what makes something fun is if you're aligned with right effort.

Complete this assignment now. Continue reading when finished.

Buddhism's Result: Freedom

Now you have completed an experiential study of the foundation of Buddhism. To further illuminate the power of these teachings, let's examine Buddhism's results. Buddhism primarily results in a reduction of egotism. Buddhism is a diet of the mind. It is a system that brings you from the excess weight of ego-clinging passions and attachments to the balanced freedom of non-addiction.

Buddhism is what I call the original twelve step program. In actuality there are not twelve steps, but Four Noble Truths plus eight folds of the path. Like the twelve step program, Buddhism brings people who are suffering from addictions through an effective regimen of disciplined steps, into a happier condition of non-addiction. Addiction is defined in Buddhism as something that we think we can't stop doing and is harmful to ourselves and others, or detracts from our happiness, peace, and well-being.

All but the Enlightened suffer addictions. We suffer addictions of seeing life in an essentially flawed way. The primary flaw in our awareness is an addiction to a self-clinging reaction to life. When we see and know life in this flawed, self-reactive way, we create our own suffering. We create and suffer addictions of thoughts, feelings, desires, and concepts. These thoughts have associated outcomes or karmas that create every aspect of our lives, even the undesirable suffering that just seems to spring up as misfortune.

The Buddha taught that we have choices. He would say, "We are what we think. All that we are arises with our thoughts. And with our thoughts, we make the world." In every moment, we are choosing our reality when we choose what to think. Our thoughts cast the deciding vote on our reality (and hanging chads do count). Buddha teaches us to understand our choices so that we can see what will bring us to true happiness.

Our minds are trapped in the illusion of the thoughts we are addicted to, the same way a crack addict is trapped by the pipe. Our minds are conditioned by the limitations of our thoughts. Just as the crack addict thinks, "I'm a good-for-nothing drug addict. I can never quit," we think, "I am this or that. I can never do this or that." We define and enforce our limitations and reality in every moment.

Why is it that we always end up in the same relationships? Or in the same situations that depress us or anger us? The answer is that we are addicted to the same relationships, depressions, and angers.

There's a joke about how we do odd things that cause our suffering. It's a joke about a man who goes over to his doctor complaining of pain. The man bends over backwards and to the side twisting his back in a strange angle and says, "Hey Doc, it hurts when I do this."

His doctor replies, "Then don't do that."

A woman attending a public meditation seminar once asked an American Zen Master, "How can I meet a good guy? All the men that I date end up being alcoholics who abuse me."

"Stop trying to get a good guy," the Zen Master answered.

Frustrated, she gave the Zen Master a questioning look.

The Zen Master went on to say, "Look, I'm going to tell you the truth and it might not be what you want to hear, but it is the way out of suffering."

She nodded.

The Zen Master continued to tell her, "Like all, you want happiness, but like so many, you go about finding it with selfish intent, producing spectacularly horrendous results."

"So what should I do?" she asked.

"First obliterate any idea of ever getting a 'good guy'. Your mind, conditioned by ignorant habits of thought, misinterprets bad for good. If you want a positive relationship, you should get a guy who is not harmful to himself or abusive to you."

The Zen Master then asked her to describe in detail a prospective guy to date who would not be harmful to himself or abusive to her.

She described a nice, handsome, and wealthy young man. She said that this man would be cultured and like the Opera. She described him as thoughtful, saying that he would buy her flowers every Saturday.

She paused for a moment with a disconcerted look. She further described that this man would never work at a job like hers, like her friends, be into the alternative music that she listened to, or hang out at the clubs she attended.

At the end of her description of a prospective date who is not harmful to himself and not abusive to her, she became flustered and said, "OK, this dream guy is nice, cute, wealthy, great, and everything, but to be really honest, we're not into the same things, and he's boring, and I really wouldn't want to date him at all!"

"So now do you understand your choice?" the Zen Master asked. She looked at him confused.

"Let me ask you a question then," he continued. "Why do you ask me how to meet a good guy when you, addicted to your suffering from bad guys, do not want to meet a good guy?"

She reflected deeply on his question. Thus her mind became clear. Her addictions and choices were revealed to her from behind her own ignorance. After a few moments of taking in the understanding that she herself chose her abusive relationships because of her own addictions to them, she let out a heavy sigh.

She paused for a moment and then said, "But these cravings and ideas have become such a strong internal definition of who I am and what I want. Truth and happiness seem so elusive and distant. What am I to do in the face of such strong addictions?"

The Zen Master responded, "Stop looking for any guy at all for a little while until you are strong enough to beat your addiction. Looking for a 'good guy' is like an alcoholic entering a bar and looking for a Coke. You really don't want a Coke. You'll never be happy with a Coke while you're suffering from your alcoholic addiction. You want a rum and Coke! However, desiring what you're addicted to only deepens your misery."

He continued, "Instead of looking for a guy, you should meditate! Stop your mind from repeating the patterns that create circumstances of suffering. Meditation will give you the strength of mind to end your addiction."

She nodded in affirmation and resolve. After a few weeks of serious meditation practice she reported to the Zen Master that she stopped hanging out at some of the clubs she used to go to.

"The only reason I went to those clubs was to find, well, my rum and Cokes," she said. The Zen Master replied, "Very good! When you avoid the places where the object of your addiction is served, your craving will soon end."

Several weeks later she told the Zen Master that she didn't even crave dating anymore. She said, "I'm happy with my life now! I feel stronger and more balanced than ever! I know that I will never have a rum and Coke again!" The Zen Master replied nodding, "Being free of your addictions is the greatest feeling in the world!"

There's another story that humorously describes the abundance of self-righteous hypocrisy that people sometimes suffer from. A man's car stalls while he is driving down the parkway. He leaves his car at the side of the road and walks one mile to a nearby auto mechanic.

He tells the auto mechanic that his car stalled making a grumbling clicking sound. The auto mechanic says, "Ah, yes of course, it's your carburetor! I've been in the auto mechanic business for over 20 years and I can recognize the description of a busted carburetor in my sleep! In fact, the carburetor in my tow truck just busted last week making the same grumbling clicking sound! And don't worry, fixing a busted carburetor shouldn't cost you more than $50 or $60 and shouldn't take more than 2 hours."

The man felt relieved that he was in good hands. He was pleased with the price estimate and the amount of time for the repair.

"Let's go walk up the parkway to where your car is," the auto mechanic said. "I'll help you push it down to the shop so I can start working on it."

"What do you mean?" the man replied. "My car is over a mile away. Can't we just drive over in your tow truck and tow my car back to the shop?"

"Heck, didn't I just get through telling you that my tow trucks' carburetor broke down last week?" the auto mechanic answered.

"Well, why didn't you fix your tow truck's carburetor?" the man asked.

"To tell you the truth," the auto mechanic said, "I don't really know how to fix carburetors so well."

"Then how do you intend to fix my carburetor?" the man asked.

"I'm not quite sure," answered the auto mechanic. "Maybe duct tape?"

A different young woman once approached a Buddhist teacher and said, "I'm seeking your advice on how I can best help the world. I feel it is my life's work to heal the sick people of this world. If I can free others from their physical suffering, I can help bring about the prophecy of a heaven on Earth."

She continued with growing exuberance, "If I and other workers of the light have helped mankind ascend high enough in consciousness, when the great astrological events occur at the end of the Mayan calendar, all of us will be transformed in the great photon beam of light that will cross this Earthly dimension and reverse the poles of our planet!

"But to be honest with you," she continued in a more deflated manner, "the reason I am seeking your advice is that I feel that my efforts so far are not having the powerful effects I desire and have read about in books. I feel like something is missing or that I'm doing it wrong because nothing is happening!"

She paused for a moment and then continued, "I find myself just hoping and hoping that all the badness in the world will just end. I hope that the books I've read and the people I've talked to are right, that the suffering of our world will end soon when a new age of light comes."

She paused for another moment with a concerned look on her face and then said, "But what if it doesn't come or I don't do what I'm supposed to in order to bring about the new age? So what I need to know is what more can I do than massage therapy and Ayurvedic medicine to help the world be free of suffering? What more can I do to bring heaven to all beings on Earth?"

The teacher nodded and told her that she understood her situation. "Many successful seekers on the spiritual path have had similar dilemmas," the teacher said. "There are powerful Buddhist teachings to aid you in finding what you seek. Would you like to learn these spiritual teachings?"

The young woman smiled and said, "Yes, I would. Thank you!"

The teacher brought her hands together and said, "If you want to relieve the suffering of people in this world and wish to bring about a heaven on Earth you should..." She paused for a moment, then leaned forward, "You should spend more time alone in nature!"

"What? I don't think I understand. How does my spending time alone in nature help relieve the suffering of people in this world and bring about heaven on Earth?" the young woman asked.

"It's simple!" the teacher answered, then asked, "When was the last time you were alone in nature?"

The young woman thought about it for a moment and said, "Well I don't go to nature very often because of my busy healing schedule downtown, but it just so happens that last week I spent several hours alone in a forest just outside of the city." She explained, "Last Sunday I had no appointments and a friend asked me to drive her out of town to the forest where she wanted to take pictures for an art project. While she spent hours taking pictures of a single tree, I hiked around alone for most of the day."

"How did you feel while alone in the forest?" the teacher asked.

"I'm not sure what this has to do with my question," the young woman responded, "but it felt pretty good. I hiked to a beautiful tree-lined lake and swam in the cool water. I found a waterfall near the lake and ate my lunch there watching the water dancing from the rocks and feeding the lake. I felt that being by the water renewed and recharged me. I then hiked to an amazing vista. I sat on some large rocks and looked down over the expansive forest. I felt alive and awake! I had a beautiful meditation there. Then I watched the most exquisite sunset! So I felt good – but what does this have to do with my question?"

"That's it!" the teacher exclaimed. "That's the answer to your question!"

The young woman raised both of her palms upward and questioned, "What is? What's the answer to my question?"

"You said that you felt renewed while alone in nature. You felt alive and awake. Isn't that the relief of suffering? Isn't your experience akin to heaven on Earth?"

The young woman shook her head, "No! No, no no no no! OK, yes, yes, I felt great going to nature. I admit that spending some time in nature made me feel better both physically and mentally than I've felt in a long time, but my question was about helping others out of their suffering! My question was about helping the world so that we all will have the experience of heaven in our daily lives here on Earth! What are the Buddha's teachings on this?"

"I surely am answering your question!" the teacher explained. "Or you might say that I don't answer questions as much as I answer people. At a deeper place than you are aware of, your spirit is asking an important question that couldn't even be put into words. I am addressing your spiritual question. Pay closer attention to the answer. I understand your question better than you do.

"Your feeling peace, renewal, and awakening by spending time alone in nature is completely congruent with what the Buddha meant when he said, 'If you really wish to help others with their suffering and Enlightenment, first you need to do something harder: help yourself.'"

The young woman looked at the teacher incredulously and said, "I asked you to give me advice on helping others and you're telling me to spend time alone in nature to help myself? That just doesn't seem right!"

The teacher answered, "Yet the fact that you have this pressing question demonstrates that there is something wrong with what seems right to you."

The young woman nodded a bit reluctantly as the teacher continued, "Now that you have the answer to your question, let's attend to why you even have the question!" The teacher paused and addressed her directly, "You are addicted to seeing yourself as a savior. And how can a savior just attend to her own Enlightenment instead of everyone else's problems? That's what just doesn't seem right from your addicted point of view."

The teacher paused. With a gesture of her hand, eliciting the young woman's undivided attention, the teacher continued, "Actually, what isn't right is that you're addicted to being a savior and yet you can't save anyone!"

The teacher giggled for a moment because the young woman was so offended by this obvious truth. The teacher then continued more empathetically, "This is why you feel so miserable. You see all of your saving efforts ultimately failing. You know deep inside that your future new age hopes and savior concepts rely on self and not on truth."

The teacher continued, "Your addiction has you in a trap. You can't escape because you think that feeding your addiction is the way out. You can't heal the world! You can't bring an experience of heaven to everyone on Earth. All of your efforts will never be enough. You can, however, end your addiction. Within your addiction you perceive conflict. Outside of your addiction lies peace. Give yourself a break. You don't have to save anyone. Just attend to yourself, your own Enlightenment."

Growing defensive, the young woman argued, "Are you saying that selfless giving is wrong? That the pathway to union through service is wrong? Are you telling me that Krishna's teachings on Karma Yoga are wrong?" By the end of speaking her questions, her voice had risen shakily, one of her fists was clenched, and she was frowning.

The teacher answered, "Not at all, but I think you are showing yourself right now that you possess a lot of egotistical reaction in association with your selfless saving. True selfless giving is giving selflessly. You are addicted to being a giver, a healer, a helper, a spiritual savior. In your addiction to conceptual spirituality and selfless giving, your ego has become bigger than someone who is not 'spiritual' and never gives to others at all."

The young woman saw her egotistical response to the teacher. She stilled her reactions and listened closely.

The teacher continued, "Anyone who feels suffering from giving is not selflessly giving. How can you say that you're a worker of the light when your mind is filled with darkness? Your acts of healing, giving, and saving for your spiritual concepts are extremely selfish acts that increase your addiction and make you miserable."

The young woman paused to take all of this in, nodded, and said, "I understand what you're telling me. But can't I help people out of their suffering exactly because of the fact that I myself am in suffering and know how terrible it is? Doesn't having that suffering allow me to be open to the suffering of others and motivate me to seek a better condition for myself and them?"

The teacher answered, "Do you know the first rule that all medical, fire, and military emergency first responders learn? They learn that before you can try to save someone else, you must make sure that you save yourself first and that you are in a strong enough position to save others. Helping others is the same in spirituality.

"You're a savior, but you yourself are drowning. At the same time you're trying to save others from drowning. This only serves to drown you faster and it doesn't really help them ultimately. I'm teaching you to swim. If you spend your energy learning to swim for yourself, then you won't drown. If you become a very strong swimmer like me, not only can you save yourself, but you may be able to save others from drowning or teach others to swim!

"It's very egotistical to think that you can help others with their spirituality when you're so spiritually confused yourself. I'll let you in on a little secret. Heaven or hell is a choice each of us makes. And you cannot make that choice for another. But you can teach them to swim!"

The young woman reflected on this teaching for a few minutes and took it to heart. She said, "I understand and I want to learn to swim well so that when I'm strong enough to save myself, I can also save others. But how do I become spiritually strong without getting mired in my addiction of saving?"

"Very good!" the teacher commented and then continued, "Spend one day a week in nature. It's a very good idea to bring a friend, but make sure that you give each other enough space for self reflection. Taking a day for your own renewal and awakening requires that you break your addictive patterns of always saving others. Spending a day alone in nature is a physical application of attention to your happiness and peace. Being alone in nature is a practice where you feel good, clear out from a week in the city, and gain bright experiences in nature. Being alone in nature is beneficial for you! Selflessly spending time and energy on doing things that are healthy and developmental for yourself will give you a practice that will lead to the end of your addiction."

The young woman understood and started her path to peace and balance.

There's a joke that describes our addictions to dissatisfaction. It is a joke about a construction worker who opens his lunch tin during his break and moans, "Gosh darn it, peanut butter sandwiches!" The next day on his break upon opening his lunch tin he again groans, "Not peanut butter sandwiches again!" Still, the next day upon opening his lunch tin, he laments, "Yuck, peanut butter sandwiches!"

A co-worker seeing him complain about his peanut butter sandwich lunch three days in a row said, "Look pal, if you don't like peanut butter sandwiches so much, why don't you tell your wife to make something else for you?"

"What do you mean?" he said to his co-worker in an annoyed tone, "I prepare my own lunch!"

Another time after an afternoon meditation seminar, a troubled young man asked the Buddhist teacher why it was that he would often be bullied and beaten up at high school parties. He added, "And I even know it's gonna happen before the party starts. I always get picked on. It's so unfair!"

The teacher told him, "You see it works like this, you are predisposed by your karma to think the thoughts you think. If you choose the easy way of engaging in your habitual thoughts, then yes, things will happen just how you expect."

"What?" he exclaimed loudly. "What are you saying? You're saying I get bullied because I'm always thinking, 'Hey, we're at a party, some big drunk football player should come over and beat me up!' And you're saying that I choose to think that!? Are you high?"

"Yes!" the teacher answered, "but it's not exactly the way you understand it."

Perplexed, the young man asked, "Well then, in what way exactly should I understand it?"

The teacher smiled and with a slow affirmative nod said, "It would be my pleasure to help you understand how to free yourself of this disturbing situation. Take comfort! I will show you the truth, so that you will never be assaulted at a party again!" The young man relaxed a little bit, smiled hopefully and nodded in agreement and acceptance.

The teacher continued, still nodding, "The main thing that you have to learn to do is stop starting all these fights."

The young man frowned and interrupted the teacher, shouting, "Are you kidding me!? I never start the fights! I don't even say or do anything! Bullies just come over to me and say 'What are you looking at dweeb!?' Or, 'You're going down nerd!' And then they hit me! I don't start the fights, I just get beaten up! I even plead with them not to hurt me! This Buddhist stuff is just crazy!"

The teacher continued nodding and said, "Yes exactly! And through these crazy teachings a smart fellow like yourself can understand the mechanics of the relationship between mental outlook and physical occurrence."

Still frowning, the young man said, "What exactly are the mechanics you're talking about?"

Maintaining his friendly smile and affirmative nodding, the teacher said, "The mechanics of life! As I said before, you have a predisposition to create your reality in a particular way. This predisposition comes from your addiction to seeing the world in a limited model based on past experience. At a point probably in your early childhood, you experienced an oppressive and bullying situation at a celebratory event." He shook his head, with a frustrated and questioning look of denial.

The teacher continued, "The experience, though you may not remember it now was so upsetting to you that you created a new equation to add to your model of life. Your new way of seeing life overwrote the balanced equation of party = fun + happiness. Because of one bad experience, you now thought: party = fun + unfair bullying. You desire the fun at parties but then are completely unbalanced by the unfair bullying. The incongruous desire for fun, and dissatisfaction of unfair bullying has made you very angry. So your predisposition of anger means that you've got a bona fide chip on your shoulder!"

The young man's frown softened and he leaned in to listen more carefully. The teacher continued, "You're like the famous small king of the North. The small king was a little guy in a land where all the people were very tall. The small king was upset because he was so short. He tried to compensate for his feelings of inadequacy by building a giant castle to live in. He also compensated for his short stature by riding in huge coaches drawn by many horses. The only problem you see is when you are upset about being small, the giant castle you build for yourself and the massive coaches you ride in just always remind you that you are indeed very small. So the small king of the North felt small and reinforced it. You're kind of the same way. You go to parties thinking that you will be unfairly bullied, and you are the one who builds your castle."

Then the young man's frown slowly faded as his jaw dropped slightly. He asked, "How..."

The teacher laughed, "Good! So now, you really want to know something. Here's how it works. Because you are addicted to the party = fun + unfair bullying equation you go to parties and constantly seek the unfair bullying. The unfair bullying thought runs beneath the surface through your mind constantly like a utility program in a computer operating system. The thought triggers feelings of unease, fear, and anger. These thoughts and feelings trigger an intense reaction in your energy body. Within the subtle physical structures of your aura, you start to feel out the energies and auras of others in the room to find an energetic match that is an acceptable equivalent to your unfair bully addiction. Once you find one or more acceptable bullies, you start antagonizing them with your anger. You feel out which buttons to push to get a bullying response from them and you push with great effectiveness.

"As you push them with your anger in their most susceptible area, you also entice them to put an end to it, and show them that you're so weak that it would be easy. In that way you're like the Black Knight in Monty Python's film *The Quest for the Holy Grail*. You've got no sword, no arms, and no legs, but angrily incite a quarrel." They both laughed about the situation in the film.

Then the teacher continued, "The physical body shows subtle signs of this as well. When you think the thoughts and have the feelings that are produced in your equation, the hypothalamus in your brain produces a specific concoction of peptides that speed through your spinal fluid and blood plasma to your cells to produce physical activity. Lie detectors can measure these physical changes. Actually people are subconsciously very aware of these physical changes too. You know sometimes when a girl likes you from maybe just a glance or a smile right? So too can a glance and the lack of a smile start a fight!"

"I see," he said, nodding.

The teacher asked, "Have you ever seen an angry guy intent on fighting?"

"Yes, at the parties where I get bullied," he answered.

The teacher asked again, "Have you ever seen a victim prior to their victimization?"

"Yes I have. I know what you mean," he answered.

The teacher continued, "Well, look at yourself in the mirror my friend, and think about going to a party tonight. You'll see both."

After speaking, the teacher continued nodding and smiling. By this time, the young man was engaged in this realization. Smiling and nodding with the teacher, he said in wonder, "I do make my own castle after all!" They looked at each other, smiling and nodding.

A moment later he asked, "Now that I know that I'm the one who created what I hated about parties, what should I do now? How do I stop starting fights?"

"I've already started you on the answer to this question. It's easy! All you have to do is just exactly what you're doing now. Smile and nod! Give everyone a genuine smile and an affirming nod. With simple attention to such positive body language, it will keep you in this awareness of how you can keep the peace and have fun!"

The young man smiled and nodded, then bowed to the teacher and left for a party.

•

Assignment: What It Means to Me

Now you have completed an experiential study of the Buddha's teachings and have examined Buddhism's results. As a conclusion and recapitulation of this study, reread your Enlightenment Journal from the beginning to your last words. From your own experience in your own life, and as written testament in your Enlightenment Journal, you have seen the truth of Buddha's teachings.

On the second page of your Enlightenment Journal entitled, "What I Want to Know," you wrote down what you hoped to learn by doing this study. Reflect on what you wanted to know and what you have learned so far.

At this time you should determine what these truths and teachings mean to you. Open your Enlightenment Journal to a new page and entitle this page, "What It Means to Me."

When learning the Four Noble Truths, realizing the Middle Way, and establishing the Eightfold Path the Buddha determined that these matters were so important that he dedicated his life to the teachings of Enlightenment.

Is what you've learned so far compelling and intriguing? Are these self-experienced insights into your life and the universe of value to you? What have you learned from this examination of the Buddha's teachings and your life? Write your observations down in your Enlightenment Journal. Write down what you've learned and what it means to you.

Complete this assignment now. Continue reading when finished.

Mystical Teachings

Now that you have learned how the Buddha's teachings apply to your life, you can learn some of the more mystical Buddhist teachings for Enlightenment. As you continue on with the study of the Enlightenment Workbook, learning the mystical pathway to Enlightenment, there will be more insightful, challenging, and Enlightening reading, as well as additional assignments to engage in and learn from.

To begin, it is important to understand what Buddhist mysticism is. Buddhist mysticism is the cultivation and use of power for the purpose of Enlightenment. Buddhist mysticism teaches you to move beyond your ego-bound habits and mundane states of consciousness. It requires a great degree of attention, discipline, and a true yearning for evolution.

From this study of Buddhist mysticism, you will create a Power Plan for your life that will be a tremendous aid to your happiness and Enlightenment. To the Buddhist mystic, gaining power and not losing power is a moment by moment practice of a strategic Power Plan that leads to Enlightened states of awareness. Living observantly in this developmental structure enables a Buddhist mystic to ascend into very high states of consciousness, happiness, and ultimately to liberation.

To better describe the study of Buddhist mysticism, I will relate an old story about a student who wanted to study with a master of mysticism. The master was on the other side of a deep and fast moving river. The student yelled across to the master, "How do I get to the other side?"

The master replied, "My son, you are already on the other side!" Buddhist mystics use humor whenever possible!

Then the student explained, "No, I want to get over to your side so that I can learn mysticism from you!"

Then the Master said, "If you want to learn mysticism from me, then from where you are standing, jump as far as you can forward and slightly to the left."

The student exclaimed, "But master, if I jump forward and to the left I'll land in the river and be swept away."

The master repeated, "If you really want to learn mysticism from me, then jump!"

The student didn't understand why the master wanted him to jump in the water and be swept away. He thought that maybe the master was perhaps testing his resolve and wanted to see if he would do all that he was ordered to do. He figured anyway, that with a little effort and luck he would be able to swim back to shore unharmed. So he decided to jump and appease the master.

He jumped as far forward as he could, and slightly to the left. He expected to splash into the water, but to his surprise his feet landed on something hard and stable just beneath the water's surface. He looked down to see that he was standing on the top of a submerged boulder that was invisible to his sight from a few feet away. The master yelled, "Good! Now jump forward and to the right, but land only on your left leg!"

The student now became a little afraid. If he jumped forward again, he'd be closer to the center of the river, where the water was very deep and ran very fast. There could be no boulder large enough to land on there. The master signaled him to jump. Although afraid, the student listened to the master and jumped just the way the master had instructed him to.

As his left foot splashed a few inches into the water he found himself miraculously supported by something that was swaying but solid. The student looked down in to the water to see that he was perched precariously on a large root of an upside-down tree. The tree must have drifted down the river and had become lodged in the large rocks at the bottom. The stable surface of the root was only big enough to fit one of his feet.

The master said, "Good! Now step to the left." The student stepped to the left and found that just beneath the surface was a rock. The master said, "Good! Now step forward and to the right." The student stepped and found a lodged log just beneath the surface. The master kept giving instructions and the student kept following the instructions and moving forward.

The student progressed and after a while learned to look beneath the surface for himself. The student was now able to see the rocks, trees, and logs beneath the surface, and no longer needed the master's instructions in order to know his next step. Finally, the student found himself reaching the other side. "This is fantastic!" he exclaimed.

Upon ascending up the river bank to where he saw the master, the student found that the reeds that the master stood in were taller than his head. Being engulfed in the reeds, the student lost sight of the master. Upon reaching the last location that he had seen the master from the river, the student looked up and saw the master above the tall reeds.

The master was floating ten feet above the ground. "You can levitate?" the student asked in wonder.

The master replied, "I had to in order to get above the reeds and see beneath the surface of the water to tell you where to step."

The master descended to the ground in a nearby clearing. The student asked, "How do you levitate?"

The master said, "In much the same way as you cross the river. You use structures that are just beneath the surface."

Just then a dozen villagers ran over to the clearing where the master and student now stood, exclaiming to the student, "How miraculous! We all saw you walking on water! You must be truly spiritually gifted!"

The student shook his head and said, "Actually, anyone can do it if you learn to look beneath the surface."

In Buddhist mysticism, a master tells a student to take actions that teach the student about other dimensions of truth, other structures of reality that are conducive to awakening and are just beneath the surface.

In Buddhist mysticism there is a need for action. Actions free you. The master knows where the invisible boulders are beneath the surface and directs physical world activities that teach you lessons of the nonphysical world. The Master can direct you to taking actions that will lead you to awareness.

In the movie The Karate Kid, the student requests to learn karate because he has a pressing need to defend himself from some kids at school. Mr. Miyagi, his sensei, agrees to teach him and begins by telling him to paint a long fence and wax several cars.

Though the kid thought that the chores were just tasks that he had to do first in order to be taught the power of karate later, it turns out that the chores themselves in fact teach him the power of karate. Tasks that sometimes seem to be unrelated to your goal, if guided by a master, can lead you to a greater awareness and power.

What Is Power?

Power is a band of awareness. There are many powers. Powers are vibrations or frequencies of life that one may perceive. It works kind of like a radio. When you're tuned into a band of awareness, you can receive information from it. All human beings alive on this planet have a certain power in common. We all have the power to perceive this world. We all perceive the same band of awareness.

It's as if we're all tuned into the same radio station. We are all able to perceive the same information, structures, and possibilities that we call life, that we call the world. All humans perceive a couple of bands of awareness: the waking band of awareness and the dreaming band of awareness. Let's call them the public radio station for waking awareness and easy listening station for dreaming awareness. These are bands around the center of the dial. Higher frequency bands have a positive effect on our consciousness, while lower frequency bands have a negative effect on our consciousness.

Some people have access to other bands of power. Some access lower bands of power. We will call them the gangsta rap stations. Some people access higher bands of power. We will call them the classical music stations. Those who engage in the gangsta rap stations will mix the violence and profanity they experience in that band of awareness into their public radio and easy listening experience. Those who can ascend to the higher classical station bring a dimension of timeless beauty to their public radio and easy listening experience.

Your awareness of the Enlightened truth of life within and throughout all bands of awareness makes up your personal power. Personal power is your personal level of spiritual power. Your level of personal power determines all that you are aware of in life, what opportunities of happiness you have, and your condition of freedom from suffering.

In Buddhist mysticism, you focus on cultivating personal power. You learn to ascend to higher bands of awareness and how to constructively deal with lower bands of awareness. By observing your own mind, life, and experience, you can increase your personal power and see your happiness and awareness of Enlightenment grow.

Power is real. Different bands of awareness offer different information, possibilities, and experiences of life. In Buddhist mysticism not only do you learn about powers that are associated with the physical world, like money, martial arts, and career success, but you also learn about powers that are associated with the nonphysical world, like dreaming, healing, and seeing. Dreams are nonphysical bands of awareness that are very real when experienced.

Nonphysical bands of awareness are unlimited because they are not bound by the physical world. Nonphysical bands of awareness can also be much more real than the physical world.

When we wake up from a bad dream we say, "Oh, it was just a dream." The dream was real to us while we were in it, but the dream was very transient compared to our waking awareness so we can set it down as being not real enough to matter. In Buddhist mysticism it is possible to wake up to other awarenesses that are much less transient than our usual waking awareness. When we wake up to these more real awarenesses, we often look at our usual waking awareness and think of it as just a dream. Compared to Enlightenment, this world we see before us is just a dream, transient and fading.

There is a nonphysical power that is more real than the physical world you see before you. Actually, it's the greatest power in the universe. When aligned with this power, you can accomplish anything. This power is called love. All Buddhist mysticism is rooted in this power.

Assignment: Proof of the Greatest Power in the Universe

Think of the people you love. Perhaps you love your mother, boyfriend, or brother? If they were troubled, in harm's way, or ill, what would you not do to help them? In the consideration of love you'll see that even impossible things in the physical world are possible to overcome. In this way love is more powerful than anything in the physical world.

Entitle a new page in your Enlightenment Journal, "Proof of the Greatest Power in the Universe."

Write down declarations of love for each person you love. State that you love them and explain why. You don't need to write a lot or to get intellectual about it. The heart often speaks in few words. Just state your love simply and completely.

Complete this assignment now. Continue reading when finished.

Assignment: I Love Me

Do you love yourself? Because of negative experiences in the past and the many hardships in life, we often get down on ourselves. Despite any difficult experiences that you've had in the past, you should embrace who you are and love yourself.

Some of us cherish our egos so much that we overlook the gentle depths of our eternal nature and celebrate the shallow characteristics of our surface form and transient experience with great hubris.

Love is the greatest power in the universe! We all have a pure, selfless love for ourselves deep down in our hearts. In the reflection of that bright and beautiful selfless love for your being, look into a mirror and say to yourself, "I love you." Say it from your heart. Say it like you mean it, and mean what you say. Say it as many times as you have to until you understand what you mean and what you're telling yourself.

Open your Enlightenment Journal to a new page and entitle it, "I Love Me!" Write about your experience.

Complete this assignment now. Continue reading when finished.

Responsibility

Love for yourself is your greatest aid for overcoming darkness and any obstacles on the pathway to Enlightenment! Love for yourself is not ego cherishing, it is the proper reflection of your life. Love for yourself initiates your responsibility for evolution. Taking responsibility for your life is the proper way to honor your love. Being responsible for your happiness in thought, word, and action in every moment is the practice of honoring your love for yourself.

Read these words silently and carefully. Listen to the words as they are enunciated in your mind. Why is your thinking voice the same as your speaking voice? Is that your true voice? Consider now who is reading, who is speaking, who is thinking? Under your habitual thoughts and speaking voice is your original voice, the eternal you, a profound and powerful awareness. That is whom I am addressing.

You are responsible for your life. You are responsible for your happiness. You are responsible for your Enlightenment. Pretending to give up your responsibility out of fear or ignorance is in the end still only exercised by you and under your authorization. There is no one else but you who has authority over your happiness. You alone command the absolute authority over your Enlightenment. There is no other authority responsible for your success or failure in life.

To succeed on the pathway of Enlightenment, you must take responsibility for your innocence and harmlessness.

Everyone in prison will tell you that they are innocent. They'll tell you that their failure was not their fault and that someone else is responsible for them not succeeding.

Criminals irresponsibly squander their innocence in the selfish ambitions of their goals. As well, criminals are sentenced to prison terms because they have committed harm to others. All beings want to be happy, but not all beings take responsibility for the innocence and harmlessness of their aspirations.

In pride, desire, and ignorance, we seek outcomes just as criminals do. Our egotistical ambitions may help us accumulate wealth and transient experiences, or achieve power and title, yet our happiness is left empty, unfulfilled in the prison of the mind.

Buddhist mystics, however, are never sentenced to the prison of the state or the prison of the mind. Although they may have many goals, their goals are conducive to awakening. In every endeavor Buddhist mystics are responsible and make innocence and harmlessness the foundation for attaining any goal.

Assignment: Goals

What are your goals and aspirations? What are the realities of your goals? Do you enjoy doing the things you have to do in order to achieve your goals?

Entitle a new page in your Enlightenment Journal, "Goals." List what your goals are. Then write down the story of how achieving each goal would most likely play out. Be realistic about how you think it would happen and if you would succeed. Consider carefully what the challenges are and how you would overcome them.

Upon completing each story, evaluate it in terms of whether the process of reaching your goals evolves you or not. Describe what you enjoy, what you love, and what is spiritually evolutionary about the process of attaining your goals.

Complete this assignment now. Continue reading when finished.

Enjoy the Process!

Buddhism is process oriented. Enjoying the process of life is the ultimate goal! Consider the old famous Zen saying, "Before Enlightenment, chop wood and carry water. After Enlightenment, chop wood and carry water." This saying wisely describes the spiritual path as a process and not an outcome.

If your goal was to eat vegan rabbit stew, you should enjoy chopping the wood for kindling the fire that you will use for cooking. You should love carrying the water that you will boil the tofu rabbit in.

On one occasion, a Zen monk was sitting in a diner in Los Angeles. His waitress was moved to tell him about her spiritual insight. She said to him, "I came to Los Angeles 12 years ago. My goal was to become a movie star. I learned one important thing about life since then. Life is what happens to you while you're waiting for your ship to come in." The monk nodded affirmingly.

The best way to be happy, whether you achieve your goals or not, is to choose goals where the process evolves you. If you enjoy the process and the hardships of working toward the goal and not just the outcome of reaching the goal then you are assured success.

Positive outcomes are fine, but if your goal is outcome-focused, beware, the ego's ambitions are the way to lose your innocence and happiness. Align yourself with what you love about the process of reaching a goal. Loving the process is where you'll achieve the goal of innocence.

No matter the facts or substance of a goal, the essence of the goal is happiness, getting higher. Choose your goals in terms of your love for the process. Goals change as you grow.

Assignment: The Meaning of Life

What is the meaning of life? The meaning of life is very similar to your goals. You choose! And what you choose as the meaning of life determines much about your experience of life.

For many people, the meaning of life consists of a conceptual religious, scientific, or societal story and a reality of desperate stuff-ism. One of the central principles of Buddhist mysticism is that you choose the meaning of life. If you think that life is a rat race, you'll probably find that you are a rat. If you think this is a dog eat dog world, you'll probably be eaten by a dog. When you take responsibility for your innocence and harmlessness, you can choose a brighter meaning and experience of life.

Open your Enlightenment Journal and entitle a new page, "The Meaning of Life." Succinctly state what the meaning of life is for you.

Complete this assignment now. Continue reading when finished.

The Use of Power for Evolution

Buddhist mystics use power to shift through states of mind and levels of consciousness. They use power to explore different dimensions of reality in order to be more aware and balanced in their lives. Buddhist mystics use power to get things and to get into situations that are helpful for their practice and conducive to awakening.

Buddhist mystics never ever use power to get ahead at the expense of another person's happiness. Power is used only to push oneself beyond one's own limitations.

Once, a devout student of a Buddhist mystic asked his teacher, "Great master, would you give me a mystical teaching to overcome my desire for worldly wealth. Although I love my spiritual studies, I still long to live in a mansion and to eat fine foods and have expensive comforts."

His teacher said, "I will give you an empowerment that will bring you tremendous wealth! You will go into the city and become a leader of industry. This empowerment will help you be very successful in all of your business dealings."

"But master," the student replied, "I want to end my desire for wealth, not become wealthy. I know nothing of business, and I'm uninterested in the business world. I don't think I'd want success even if empowered."

His master replied, "Yet you are not mature enough to know that wealth won't bring you happiness. Experience this dimension of life and you will learn a profound spiritual lesson! In the business world you will gain the power of wealth. You must master this power and remain selfless to attain liberation. It all begins with this empowerment!"

The student agreed and was empowered. He soon became a wealthy businessman. This lesson brought him beyond his desire. Sitting in his lavish mansion in the midst of his comforts he attained Enlightenment.

Assignment: My Description of Self

Who are you? Note the following attributes about yourself. Accurately answer each of the following questions. Entitle a new page in your Enlightenment Journal, "My Description of Self." Write down the answers to the questions right now, just after you read them.

What is your name?
What is your age?
What is your gender?
What high school did you go too?
What kind of music do you like?
What sports or physical activities do you enjoy?
How many push-ups can you do?
What are your hobbies?
What is your favorite food?
What is your job?

You can use power to move beyond the limited self. You can be more than you think! You can use your power to be more than this definition. Use your power to push beyond this definition of who you are. Please recall the part of your definition that states how many push-ups you can do. To make sure that your answer is accurate, do as many push-ups as you can now and note the number.

For this assignment, work up to exceeding that number of push-ups by ten additional push-ups. Try everyday until you can do ten push-ups more than the number of push-ups you can do now. Push yourself to do ten more push-ups.

You should continue with the Enlightenment Workbook while you work on this assignment everyday.

Your description of yourself does not truly describe who you are. Your power to push yourself beyond your limits describes who you are more accurately. When you complete this assignment, you will be a stronger person. You will have used your power to push yourself to new capabilities. You will have changed and grown. Your old description of self will no longer be valid.

Proof that You're Psychic

Rapid psychic development is an essential discipline for beginning Buddhist mystics. The truth is, if you've made it this far in this book, you are most likely psychic. This is an important thing for you to realize, because you cannot practice Buddhist mysticism unless you are psychic.

A lot of people who are psychic just don't know it, because being psychic is really no big deal. You just know when your best friend is going to call on the phone, you just know what food your body needs to be healthy, you just know what streets are safe to walk down, and what people mean despite what they say.

Psychic people also often get really confused. They cannot tell what thoughts are theirs and what thoughts originate from other people. Thoughts are vibrations, and psychic people resonate with the vibrations within them, but also with vibrations outside of them. Whether or not the thought originates within you, since you are psychic, you are affected by it.

Many psychic people, when not having a structured study for spiritual development, often find themselves acting out what others think, but find themselves desperately unfulfilled. Some psychic people frustrate and confuse other people because, operating with additional subtle information, they often do things that seem illogical and odd to others.

There is an old Star Trek episode where a passenger who is psychic joins the Starship Enterprise as it travels to Spock's home planet, Vulcan. The passenger tells Captain Kirk that he really needs to get psychic training from the Vulcan mind masters.

Captain Kirk asks him why he wants to learn to be psychic and read people's minds. The passenger tells Captain Kirk that he does not want to learn to be psychic and to read people's minds. He says that he already is too psychic. His problem is that he has no peace of mind because he absorbs everyone's thoughts around him.

The passenger tells Captain Kirk that he wants to learn from the Vulcan mind masters how not to be so psychic. He wants to control his psychic sensitivity so that he can be at peace and use his psychic powers more positively.

Assignment: Proof That I'm Psychic

Entitle a new page in your Enlightenment Journal, "Proof That I'm Psychic."

Go out to nature. Go to a park or a beach far from people. Go to the most beautiful place in nature that you can reach in about an hour. Spend an hour or so in nature. Write down your thoughts and how you feel.

Immediately after spending time in nature, go directly to Ikea, Wal-Mart, Kmart, or a similar discount mega-store. Spend an hour there. Write down your thoughts and how you feel. Don't get involved in shopping. Just observe your mind, thoughts, and feelings.

If you're psychic you'll notice that in Ikea you have more thoughts and that many of your thoughts are not very bright. On the other hand, in the place of nature far from people, you'll notice that you have far fewer thoughts, and that the thoughts you do have are more positive.

Complete this assignment now. Continue reading when finished.

The Past Is Dust

Everyone alive experiences suffering and pain. Although we may sympathize with the woes of others, their suffering doesn't pinch like our own sorrows. We need to relieve the pinching that causes us so much pain. When we look carefully at our pain, we often see that we are the ones doing the pinching. In the past when we felt harm, we reacted by pinching the wound to attend to the hurt. Long after the pain of the wound is gone, we're still pinching the wound, preventing it from healing and causing ourselves prolonged anguish.

It is as if we are balloons. We want to fly into the heavens, yet we hold onto many weighted lines. The weights are our past woes and past pains, our past angers and past depressions. Holding on to the lines keeps our current awareness connected to our past suffering. These weighted lines hold us down only because we hold onto them.

Not only do the lines keep us from flying, but we also exhaust ourselves expending great amounts of energy holding on to the lines. We don't know how to let go of our past suffering though our past suffering depletes us and holds us down. In Buddhist mysticism we learn to let go of the weighted lines of past sorrows that keep us from flying. Free from past injury, you can fly swiftly to the heavens with nothing left to pull you down.

First you must release what makes you mad, angry, and upset.

A Zen story tells of two monks walking on the path to their monastery, retuning from the village. They came across a beautiful woman adorned in a silk kimono. The woman stopped, unable to cross a large muddy puddle obstructing the path without dirtying her fine clothing. The younger Zen monk seeing her dilemma, offered his service, picked her up and carried her across the muddy puddle. The older monk was shocked and outraged. Touching a woman was against a monk's vows!

The woman thanked the young monk and they walked on. An hour or so later as the two monks neared the monastery, the older monk, unable to keep his composure, burst out saying, "I can't believe you! You held a woman! That is against your vows as a monk!"

The younger monk responded, "I put her down an hour ago. Why are you still holding her?"

The younger monk had a wise lesson for the older monk. Similarly to the older monk in the story, in your past there were pressure points, emotional events that ruined your peace and made you very upset. These were powerful events that affected you with strong negativity. These are events that really snagged your soul and imbalanced you.

In Buddhism we say that difficult people, painful experiences, and sorrowful situations are like gurus because we can learn the most challenging lessons in life from them. These emotional pressure points are lessons that you have not yet learned. You can tell because you're still stuck on them. They remain in your mind as unresolved issues.

A woman once approached her Buddhist teacher seeking freedom from the suffering of her past. She said to her teacher, "I was raped by my father when I was young. Of all the experiences in my life, this is the thing that I am most hurt about. Can you help me free myself from this pain?"

Her teacher listened with great care and responded, "You were hurt, and hurts can be healed. I will help you heal your hurt in time. But before we can heal the hurts of the past, we must stop the angers of the present."

The woman consented with a nod and listened attentively for her teacher's insights. He looked her directly in the eyes and said, "The problem is that you're a victim and not a survivor."

Her teacher paused thoughtfully for a moment and then explained, "A victim is someone who is being afflicted now. A survivor is someone who has made it beyond affliction. You were victimized by your father long ago. Now you victimize yourself with your own anger about the past."

The woman brought herself to nod in acknowledgement of this truth. Her teacher continued, "Your past victimization was such a terrible experience that it engendered your reactions of anger. Now the hurt is locked behind a wall of complex angry reactions. Your anger cherishes your hurt. Your anger cannot exist without your hurt. Your greatest hurt now is your anger. This reaction makes it impossible for you to heal."

Frustrated, the woman said, "I was put through hell when I was only six years old! What do you expect?"

Her teacher replied, "Nothing. It's not your fault that you were victimized. And you reacted as best you could at the time."

He leaned closer to her and said, "However, now I shall impart to you the spiritual secret of dissolving all anger, dissolving this painful obstacle to your healing."

Raising his left pointer finger her teacher exclaimed, "Forgiveness!"

Lowering his hand, he continued, "Buddhists always forgive, but never forget!"

Her teacher further explained, "Forgiveness is the means by which we detach ourselves from the suffering of anger. We yield our self focused reactions of anger to our Enlightened nature, the force of liberation from all afflictions. While we always let go of anger, we never forget what drove us to anger. Never forgetting means that we learn vital lessons of how not to be victimized again by our own anger."

Her teacher continued, "When you do not forgive, you are forever bound within the thing that hurt you and made you angry. When you forgive you are free from anger and what caused you hurt. When you forgive you become a survivor!"

He continued, "Once you have survived the onslaught of affliction, you can heal. It's impossible to heal injuries of the soul while you continue the affliction upon yourself."

She nodded as her teacher further explained, "A survivor is strong! The sorrowful experiences of the dark compel survivors to evolve in light. Being forever imprinted by the dark, a survivor gains a profound wisdom of life."

Her teacher looked her directly in the eyes as if speaking to her soul and said, "Now is the time to let go of the past. Let go of your anger. Forgive your father. Forgive yourself. Forgive and know peace. Be a survivor!"

She was instantly filled with forgiveness and empty of anger. Thanking her teacher she said, "For the first time since I was six, I feel at peace."

Buddhism is a survival game! Buddhists learn to move beyond all of the snags in life. On the pathway to Enlightenment we often fall down. Many things in life cause hurt. Instead of reacting in anger and being snagged by them, Buddhists learn the reaction of forgiveness to move beyond them.

In Buddhism what's important is that you learn the art of getting back up. What is important is the path to liberation. When you fall, simply get back up, dust yourself off, and continue on the pathway to Enlightenment. Only survivors live in peace. When you learn to yield all angers and all upsets to forgiveness you learn how to be a spiritual survivor.

The Buddha said, "Look how he abused and beat me, how he threw me down and robbed me. Live with such thoughts and you live in hate. Look how he abused and beat me, how he threw me down and robbed me. Abandon such thoughts and live in love. For in this world hate has never yet dispelled hate. Only love dispels hate. This is the law, ancient and inexhaustible."

Assignment: Upsets

Face the dark side of the self. As if you were a deep well of water, we will cast the light of truth into your depths. As we illuminate the dark shadows of the self, we reveal that, in the light of truth, the shadows vanish.

Face hate and anger. Entitle a new page in your Enlightenment Journal, "Upsets." Write down what you hate, what makes you angry and frustrated. Write down your biggest angry upsets so that you can then let go of them. Begin by reviewing your list of upsets in the "What Really Gets My Goat" assignment.

Write down the stories of the experiences that made you angry or very upset. Write out these stories in detail. After your stories of hates, angers, and upsets are written, we will transform them into understanding. Buddhist mystics use something we call "shields" to deflect and transform the darkness and negativity in our own minds. You will use one of Buddhism's most powerful shields - the shield of forgiveness. At the end of writing each story of upsetting experiences write these words: "I forgive you."

Complete this assignment now. Continue reading when finished.

Assignment: Inspirations

Let's now face jealousy. There is a mystical truth of jealousy and inspiration. Whatever you are jealous of, you block yourself from having. Whatever inspires you in others brings you closer to having yourself.

Entitle a new page in your Enlightenment Journal, "Inspirations." Write down every jealousy you have. After you've written that jealousy, find a way to be inspired by the very thing that makes you jealous.

Now turn your jealousy into an inspiration. Write down your inspiration, and then cross out the preceding jealousy statement with a big X.

Keep in mind that some of the upsets that you have already identified may also have a dimension of jealousy that you should also address with this assignment.

Complete this assignment now. Continue reading when finished.

Healing Emotional Sores by Changing the Past

We have identified and transformed your angry upsets and jealousies. We have put down your negative reactions to the past. Now we are going to look at and heal where those dark sides of the self came from.

Hate comes from hurt. Anger is a reaction to pain. Mean people, beneath their meanness, are hurt people. Anger, resentment, and hate all originate with one's own hurt. The second part of "The Past is Dust" lesson is to heal hurts of the past.

Everyone has emotional sores. They were caused in the past and remain festering in our minds. Because the sores hurt so much we are constantly guarding them in a defensive stance against life. We lament the suffering of the past and fear more infliction in the future. We spend so much energy holding onto past events that caused us harm and shielding ourselves from the uncertainty of the future, that our awareness of this moment is hindered.

Buddha told a story that reminded his students that, though the past may be terrible and the future unsure, they should be unhindered in the enjoyment of life in this moment.

Buddha said, "A man was walking across a field and encountered a ferocious tiger. He fled, with the tiger chasing after him. Coming to a cliff, he caught hold of a wild vine and swung himself over the edge. Now the man was clinging to a vine halfway down a high cliff. The tiger sniffed at him from above. Terrified, the man looked down to where, far below, another tiger had come, waiting to eat him if he fell. Now two mice crawled out of a hole in the cliff and began to gnaw away at the vine. Just then the man saw a luscious strawberry growing near him in the side of the cliff. Grasping the vine in one hand, he plucked the strawberry with the other. With a sublime smile he enjoyed the sweet taste."

The primary reason that people get emotional sores is because they get hurt by other people. Chuang Tzu, an Enlightened master tells a story of a time when he was a young man fishing in his small boat on the river. He felt great peace and had caught enough fish to feed himself for three days.

All of a sudden, his peace was ruined! A very large river ship crashed into him from behind. His fish were flung back into the water. The hull of his skiff was cracked and water was leaking in.

Chuang Tzu was furious and filled with self-pity! He looked up to the captain's chamber on the large boat and cried, "Why! How could you? I am but a poor man with a small boat! Now my fish are gone, my boat needs repair, and I won't have a meal tonight! What have you to say, for the wrong that you have done! Nothing? Now, you are really making me mad! It was your fault! I deserve an apology! You get down here right now, and help me plug the leak you caused! No? Then I'm coming up there with my fishing rod! And I'm going to teach you ignorant jerks a lesson!"

With his eyes tearing, his fishing rod in one hand and a paddle in his other hand, Chuang Tzu somehow managed to climb into the large boat. Upon bursting into the captain's chamber he held his fishing rod out and paddle high in the air only to find that no one was there. "Where are you!" he yelled. Chuang Tzu ran throughout the ship looking for someone to blame and to paddle, but he found no one.

While looking for the captain at the back of the vessel, he noticed that the mooring line, which is used to tie the ship up to a pier, was snapped in half. Realizing that no person crashed into him and that it was just the boat that crashed into him, Chuang Tzu dropped all of his anger and self pity.

"That's silly," Chuang Tzu thought, "I was about to smack somebody with a fishing rod and cry myself to sleep, but now that I know there is no person responsible for the accident, I have no anger and no sorrow. Surely I should have not been upset even if there was a person intending to ram me!"

He tied a rope to his skiff and captained the large river boat to a nearby pier where he tied it up for the owner to redeem. He then started preparing his own boat. That night the pier master, inspired by Chuang Tzu's good nature offered him a lavish feast.

Most of our emotional sores come from our love for other people. We have the disposition of love for all men and women. In our heart of hearts we wish to share our love, be accepted, and be united with all others. This makes us open to others. This makes us vulnerable.

It is because we are vulnerable to and seek unity with others that we are so deeply wounded when another, out of ignorance, malice, or fear, causes us harm. In reaction to the wound, we guard the sore to keep it from any further harm. As a result of our defensiveness, though we think we are keeping the wound safe from harm, we are actually preventing it from healing. In love there is pain and sadness. Pain and sadness are what make love mature, complete, and precious.

Immature in love, always defending the pain and sadness of our sores, we drive ourselves into great suffering and quiet desperation. It is only in the consideration of love that we find the cure for our past hurts.

Assignment: Rewriting the Past

This assignment offers you a mystical medicine that will heal the emotional sores of your past! In Buddhist mysticism we call this kind of medicine "Rewriting the Past."

Most people see that by acting now, we can change the future. In Buddhist mysticism you can also act now to change the past.

First you must learn something about light, the primary ingredient in Buddhist magic. In Buddhist mysticism we often work with light to create Enlightening effects in our lives and in the lives of others. There are countless dimensions of intelligent and loving light that are accessible through special meditations and reflections.

These dimensions of light can be applied to dark areas of your life, and even to experiences of suffering in your past. Experiencing these dimensions of light makes you brighter! Experiencing these dimensions of light makes the darkness of your wounds vanish like shadows in the noon sun. Experiencing these dimensions of light makes you more Enlightened.

I will introduce you to one of these powerful dimensions of light now in order to heal you of past sorrows. Keep in mind that some of the upsets and jealousies that you have already identified may also have a dimension of hurt that you should also address with this assignment.

There is a bright white light that heals all of the suffering and pain of the past. This light is invoked by using the Sanskrit word *Om*. This white light originates in your heart chakra.

When you bring to mind places of hurt in your past and invoke the white light from your heart by saying *Om*, the light fills your memory of the past. You see the events that caused you pain in this wise light of healing.

In the presence of this white light shining like a star from your heart, your pain is healed. You are healed in the maturity of a deeper and more complete love for life. The people and events that have hurt you become bright and harmless in the light. The pain that you feel is transformed into wisdom and love.

Rewriting the past is a detailed recapitulation of past events combined with the addition of this dimension of Enlightened awareness. With Enlightened awareness a pressure point of hurt can be transformed into a catalyst for awakening.

Write your stories of past harm. Write your stories of past pain. Write all details, events, people, feelings, and what you now understand about it and think. Entitle a new page in your Enlightenment Journal, "Rewriting the Past" and write these stories out in detail.

After writing everything about the past infliction, read through the story invoking the light. In the white light of your heart, speak "*Om.*" Surround the bad parts of your experiences with light. Apply the white light of *Om* to all the people and feelings and events. Fill them with this light of benevolence.

Let go of the pain. Let go of bitterness. Be filled with forgiveness. See the you who is hurt disappear in the light. Now who is left to be hurt? At the end of each story, write the word *Om* or the Sanskrit Om symbol:

This seals the light within your past.

Complete this assignment now. Continue reading when finished.

Relationships

There's a saying that people will do the craziest things for love. In intimate relationships most people often do crazy things, but not for love. They do crazy things for desires and attachments. And that's just plain crazy!

A lot of people get hurt in intimate relationships. People also disempower themselves by spending a lot of time and energy seeking intimate relationships.

Society sells a story that the pinnacle of experience is finding the perfect relationship. Religious custodians enforce this view within the communities of their faiths. New-Agers spiritualize this story by ornamenting the intimate partner as a "soul-mate."

Many people work themselves up into a frenzied drama of going to clubs and parties, preparing their pitch and game, dressing, doing make-up, doing hair, and always looking and hoping for a mate.

People want others to love them. In Buddhism we learn that others loving you won't make you happy. You should love! That will make you happy. Buddhists work on loving instead of working to get someone else's love. That way, love is not a capricious gamble, but a conscious and happy practice that is up to you.

Buddha was not too hot on the idea of intimate relationships. He marks his own intimate relationships as being the greatest barriers to his Enlightenment. The most rules that the Buddha had for his male students were in regards to conduct with women. On top of that, for his female students, the Buddha had twice as many rules regarding conduct with men.

The Buddha believed that relationships cause tremendous egotistical attachments, desires, and fears. He thought that such transient and capricious engagements should not be clung to so dearly for happiness and fulfillment.

Relationships are of course fine to have, but not to expect or base your happiness on. Instead, base your happiness on your intimate relationship with life. If you are truly happy and free, intimate relationships don't evoke egotistical clinging, attachments, and fears. If you are truly happy and free, intimate relationships add to your joy of life.

The Transient Lifecycle of Relationships

Consider what people commonly experience while they are involved in intimate relationships. Reflecting on this subject from the point of view of Buddhist mysticism, we can identify four distinct phases.

The first phase of a relationship is called the Romantic Period. Romance is one of the most treasured experiences according to societal stories. Romance is generally confined to the first part of a relationship.

Romance is an illusion. People usually meet, fall into this grand illusion called romance and experience exhilarating joy for a short time. Though an illusion, the Romantic Period truly graces an opportunity for love. Accordingly in this birth of possibility there is a strong momentum of selflessness. The Romantic Period is sweet because, here, people let loose the grip of egotistical attention and are more focused on another's well-being. For a time there is an innocent purity. The Romantic Period usually lasts for about six months. It could be greatly shorter or perhaps twice as long depending on the power of the illusion.

The illusion is caused by the fulfillment of an energetic agreement between two auras that satisfies certain parameters of subtle physical desires. Six months later the illusion starts to fade. Just like your experience drinking water, the sweet taste starts to fade and you start to figure that the other person is not as exciting as you first thought.

This is when you enter the second phase of relationships, the Dominance Period. After six months to a year, the person who was at one time the most perfect and wonderful thing in your life starts getting on your nerves. You start noticing a thing or two about him or her that doesn't make you so happy. Here is where your initial selflessness is interrupted by older patterns of egotistical selfishness. This is where the person who could do no wrong starts doing wrong in your opinion.

After a few more months the illusion is completely gone. Now your energetic desire has been fulfilled and is satiated. Through the excitement of the initial illusion you have written intentions of connection. These attachments alone can hold a relationship together for a lifetime.

This is where you really start dealing with your intimate partner as he or she really is. This is where you really start to have an opportunity to build a mature love. Here most often, the flowers of mature love grow hindered by the weeds of selfish attachments.

Here, as the ego emerges from the selflessness of the Romantic Period, a power struggle begins. One person in the relationship will end up with power over the other person. Often but not always, it's the man over the woman. In the Dominance Period the man tries to control the woman and the woman tries to invisibly manipulate the man.

The more powerful of the two wins and becomes the dominant, freer, less giving, more taking, and happier one in the relationship. This phase usually lasts between three and six years.

The third phase of relationships is called the Relational-Self Period. In this phase, your description of yourself becomes synonymous with the description of your relationship. While this is considered to be a great success according to societal stories, in Buddhist mysticism it is seen as a tremendous delusion and obstacle to happiness.

Your description of the world is immersed in another's description. Your story together becomes foremost in the way you see life. When you think of yourself, you think of you, your intimate partner, and the matters of the relationship you've constructed. This is when you can't really see yourself being without the other. This is when you might not be happy together, but the primary description of your world is that you're just together.

In the midst of love and attachments, people become bound together for evolving and destructive reasons. In the Dominance Period love and hate often grow simultaneously. The Dominance Period carries on and deepens as long as the relationship lasts.

The fourth phase of relationships is called the Ending Period. All relationships come to an end by choice or by death. Even if you have the "perfect" relationship, in the end, just as you were born alone, you will die alone. The Ending Period can occur at any time after the Romantic Period has been initiated.

The Ending Period is often filled with sorrow and bitterness. This phase can be dragged on for months or even years. Often there is an intense egotistical reaction and great suffering at the ending of an intimate relationship.

Assignment: Relational Study

Create a new Enlightenment Journal entry entitled, "Relational Study."

Consider five couples you know and five couples you don't know. For each couple, study the following attributes:

- What phase of the relationship lifecycle are they in?
- Who is the dominant one?
- What are their conditions of love and attachment?
- Are these people really fulfilled?

For the five couples you know, if you are in a relationship, you should enter yourself and partner as one of the couples. If your mother and father are together or if you can remember their relationship, you should use your parents as another couple.

For the five couples you don't know, you may not be able to ascertain all of the study points. However, it's surprising what you can tell about a couple just by watching them shop in a store for a few minutes! Just observe these couples for a short while in a public place and see what you come up with.

Document your findings.

Complete this assignment now. Continue reading when finished.

Taking Stock of Your Power

People often get caught up in the things in their lives and get confused about what is right and what will make them happy. Taking stock of your power will give you a clear pathway to what is right for you and what will make you happy.

A young woman who had been attending weekly meditations at a Buddhist school approached the teacher to ask about a pressing dilemma. "My long-time boyfriend Daniel has just asked me to marry him." She said, "He's working in New York and just got a big promotion. He says that he's at a point in his career now that he's ready to settle down with me, buy a house, and start a family."

She went on, "I'm really happy that he got the promotion and I'm completely flattered that he proposed."

She paused with a look of concern and then said, "It's just that I've very recently been accepted into law school at Stanford. Becoming a lawyer has been a dream of mine since high school. I feel torn between marrying Daniel and following my personal ambition."

"In order to determine what is spiritually powerful for you," the teacher said, "let's consider both what is right and what will make you happy."

The young woman nodded.

"Is it right that Daniel waited until he felt he was in a strong position in his career before deciding to marry you and settle down?" the teacher asked.

"Yes," the young woman answered, "I believe so."

"In your relationship," the teacher asked, "is it right for your career aspirations to be considered equal?"

"Yes," the young woman answered, "I believe so."

"Then give yourself that right," the teacher said. "Getting to a strong point in a career is not only right for Daniel, it's right for you!"

The young woman smiled confidently.

"OK, now let's talk about what would make you happy," the teacher said. "Would you feel happy and fulfilled turning down Stanford law, moving to New York, and starting a family with Daniel?

The young woman furrowed her brow.

"Would you feel happy and fulfilled going to Stanford law, passing the BAR, and becoming an attorney?" the teacher asked.

Her brow relaxed. She paused for a moment then said, "Though I love Daniel a lot, what would bring me fulfillment right now is to go to Stanford law."

The teacher nodded, saying, "What is right and makes you happy is most powerful for your spirit."

Taking stock of your power can give you insight into what is Enlightening for you. When taking stock of your power, you consider the conditions of your life in a detached and loving way. This helps you cut to the truth of the matter to identify the important factors for your happiness.

Once at a public meditation, a young man asked a Buddhist teacher, "What should I do to avoid flunking out of school? I've recently started a certificate program at a technical trade school so that I can get a better job and get out of working with all my high school buddies at Target. But my grades are bad and I'm having trouble keeping up with my studies."

"Why is that?" The teacher asked, "Is it because you don't understand the instructor or the material?"

"No," the young man answered, "I have no problem understanding the instructor, and I can follow the material in class. I guess my problem is more that I'm having trouble studying at night and doing my homework."

"Why is that, since you said you are able to keep up in class?" the teacher asked.

"I guess it's my friends," the young man answered. "They come over every night after our shift at Target and we hang out for a couple hours. After they go home, I'm pretty tired and find it difficult to study and do homework, so I usually watch TV and then go to sleep."

The teacher nodded and said, "I understand your dilemma, and it's easy for you to fix your problem!"

The young man smiled and asked, "What should I do?"

"Stop hanging out with your friends after work and study," the teacher answered.

The young man frowned saying, "But my friends and I have hung out after work since the end of high school. And they all come to my apartment because I have the biggest living room, so it would be impossible for me to not hang out with them."

"Listen," the teacher said, "your friends are fine to hang out with after work if you don't want to increase your personal power to get a better job, but if you want to make a jump to a more powerful position in life, you will need to focus on your studies. Your technical studies are the doorway to a more powerful career. Your friends drain your power and are the obstacle to your career success."

"Maybe I can hang out with them for just 30 or 45 minutes and then go to my room to study," the young man said.

"You have a fixed window of time for your studies," the teacher said. "And you only have a certain amount of energy and clarity of mind to study. If I were you, right after your work, I'd go to the computer lab at school, a library, a study group, or to a classmate's house to focus on the most powerful thing for your life right now, gaining a stronger career."

The young man agreed. He told his friends that he would need to focus on his studies and that they couldn't hang out at his apartment after work for awhile. His friends were dismayed but accepting, knowing that his school was a positive thing for his life. The young man caught up with his studies and excelled in his classes. One year later he quit working at Target and landed a great job in his technical field.

When you take stock of your power you not only see what to do, but you see what not to do. When you clearly look at your options for power and happiness, your path becomes clear.

Once, a woman approached her Buddhist teacher to ask for advice regarding her situation at work. She said, "I've been working as a middle manager at a large company for over ten years. Some executives above me want me to be fired for political reasons and fight me in every one of my new initiatives. Also there are some young analysts below me who are broad-siding me because they are gunning for my position. I feel attacked from all sides. I've been fighting for my job and for advancement, but I fear I'm losing and will be demoted or fired. What should I do to succeed in my work?"

Her teacher said to her, "Your work place has become a very negative and disempowering place for you. The powerful thing for you to do is find another job. Then you'll be much happier!"

The woman rebutted, "I'm no quitter. I don't want to give up the fight when I know I'm in the right! Isn't it more powerful to fight against oppression and succeed with the might of your will and knowledge?"

Her teacher replied, "Fighting to win is not the point. Your happiness is. This is an endeavor that would offer little happiness even if you win. Winning would take a tremendous amount of energy. Why not stop fighting at your workplace and spend your extra energy finding a new job. In a new job, where the upper executives respect your experience and where analysts below support you, you'll profit greatly in happiness. Think things through for yourself: Which way will make you happier and more empowered?"

The woman thought for a moment and then answered, "I wouldn't ordinarily even consider giving up in a tough situation at work. However, when I contemplate the merits of finding a new job, I have to admit that it would offer me greater happiness and perhaps even more opportunity."

She paused for a moment and then continued, "I didn't consider my position in this way. I guess instead of just fighting to win, I should choose the battles that will win me happiness."

When you practice taking stock of power, you learn how to find balance while engaging in relationships, groups, and society. You learn how to participate and gain the strengths and benefits of being with others, while not being unbalanced by them or letting them affect your power negatively.

Once in a Zen center near San Francisco, an upset student approached his Buddhist teacher. He said to his teacher in an aggravated tone, "Master, I have a problem, and I need your advice to come up with a resolution! I lent my Lotus Sutra to Corbin even though he still hasn't returned the Heart Sutra that he borrowed from me two weeks ago. OK then, Corbin told me that Jean took the Lotus Sutra from him and then later let Agnot borrow it. Agnot lent it to Cornelius and Cornelius lent it to Rod. Rod said that he thought he had returned it to Corbin, but Corbin says that he never got it back! What should I do? Should I hold Corbin responsible or Rod responsible?"

His Buddhist teacher replied, "Hold yourself responsible! You are the only one responsible for your power and happiness."

The student sighed and looked dejected. His teacher continued, "I know you're trying to be nice and to help others, but it doesn't help them if you become upset allowing them to be sloppy with your aid. It doesn't help them if you allow them to disempower you. Moderate the situation so that you can help them and not get bent out of shape for it. Help them in a way that allows you to maintain your power."

"How do I do that?" the student asked.

His teacher replied, "Perhaps let Corbin read your sutras only while you are present. That way he will respect the opportunity more and you are sure to get your sutras back. In this way you can help a friend and be happier for it!"

Taking stock of your power is using common sense. We often lack common sense when we get caught up and confused in the different situations in our lives. Attachments and desires only serve to further perplex us. In general, we tend to over-think things and situations. However, one doesn't have to think much to reveal common sense. Common sense is intuitive.

On another occasion, an Enlightened Indian Yogi was meeting with his students. One of his students asked his teacher, "Guru, I have just moved into a new apartment situated one floor above an auto mechanic shop. I love the apartment, but the noise of the cars and trucks being repaired is so loud that I can't concentrate during my meditation practice. What should I do?"

The teacher asked his most advanced student, "What do you think he should do?"

The most advanced student replied, "You should meditate so perfectly that nothing can disturb your concentration."

The teacher then asked his oldest student, "What do you think he should do?"

The oldest student replied, "You should ask yourself the question, 'Who is the one who can't concentrate?' In this contemplation you will find there is no you. Then there will be no dilemma!"

The teacher said, "OK, you have your answer."

The student, a little confused, asked his teacher, "Guru, I was given two techniques. Which one shall I practice first?"

The teacher replied, "It doesn't matter! As soon as you move the hell out of that apartment you can practice either technique first."

To know what is right for yourself in life, and to learn the mystical pathway to Enlightenment you must take stock of your power. Everything in your life either gives you power or takes power away from you. Everything in your life either gives you light or gives you darkness. Everything in your life either adds to your happiness or takes away from your happiness.

What gives you power? What are the things that make you happy? What are the things that make you healthy? What evolves you? What brings you light?

What takes your power away? What are the things that make you unhappy? What are the things that make you unhealthy? What does not evolve you? What brings you darkness?

Evaluating everything in your life in these terms will show you a clear path to power, happiness, and light.

It is difficult for us to look at the things in our lives in such simplistic terms as empowering and disempowering. We don't want to accept that complex things can be viewed with such simplicity. We like to consider things from many sides. Many of the things in our lives have thousands of dimensions to them. Our rational mind wants to evaluate each aspect and become lost in the incongruities of the details.

We like to consider that, while something could be very bad, there could also be something very good about it. While another thing could be very good, there could also be something very bad about it. Things can't be so black and white. There are a lot of grey areas in life. Right?

This is all true of course from a rational perspective, but let's consider another perspective. This perspective is deeper, wiser, and yet still congruent with the essential aspects of rationality. This perspective is the perspective of the simple truth of life, the perspective of the heart.

It's hard for people to see things so simply, but in truth, at the heart of all matters, things are very simple. You might say that the heart sees in black and white.

To the heart there is either love or no love. To the heart there is either truth or obscuration. In Buddhist mysticism we learn to see our lives from a deeper place than our rational cognitive mind. We learn to see our lives from the heart. From the heart, you can look at a relationship or dilemma in your life that has hundreds of related dramas, thoughts, intentions, and feelings, and yet from a heart view, you can know if it is good overall, healthy overall, and empowering overall.

Evaluation of power in your life must come from a wiser consideration than your thinking mind. Evaluation of power must come from a healthy and bright feeling in your heart.

Taking Stock of Your Relationships

Begin by considering the relationships you have. Take stock of your current relationships. Carefully examine each of your relationships. Which ones are positive and healthy? Which relationships are negative and unhealthy? The people closest to you have the most powerful effect on you.

If you were walking down the street and a woman who is a stranger to you approached you and said, "You disgust me!" you would probably think, "That's odd. I hope she's OK," keep walking, and never think about the incident again.

But if you were walking down the street and your own mother approached you and said, "You disgust me!" you would probably think many thoughts with great concern. It would be something that bothered you for a long time.

The people closest to you, the people who know you the best and who have known you the longest, can most profoundly help you into the light, but can also profoundly hold you away from light. Consider Siddhartha's father, wife, courtesans, and best friend. This is why Buddha said, "Keep company with the holy and seekers of truth. If no others around you seek truth, then go on alone." And that is what the Buddha did.

If you find that you have negative relationships, make them positive or end them. Cut your losses if you cannot draw a profit. Draining relationships are the biggest reason why people don't succeed on the spiritual path. In most cases, negative relationships drain 85% of a man's spiritual energy and 100% of a woman's spiritual energy.

Assignment: The Power of My Relationships

Entitle a new page in your Enlightenment Journal, "The Power of My Relationships." Divide the page into two columns. Write "Relationships That Increase My Power" as the heading for the first column. Write "Relationships that Decrease My Power" as the heading for the second column. List all the relationships you have in the appropriate column.

Complete this assignment now. Continue reading when finished.

Assignment: Things That Affect My Power

Now that you know how your relationships affect your power, consider everything else in your life. What else gives you power? What else takes power away?

Entitle a new page in your Enlightenment Journal, "Things That Affect My Power." Divide the page into two columns. As the heading for the first column, write "Things That Increase My Power." As the heading for the second column, write "Things that Decrease My Power."

List all of the things in your life in the appropriate columns. List your job, your school, your hobbies, and your hang-outs. List your neighborhood, the stores you shop at, and your usual mode of transportation. List your chores, your commitments, and your common errands. List your diet, your sleep, and your exercise. List what you do on an average day. List the things you do with your free time, the things you do to have a good time, and the things you don't like to do yet find yourself doing. List the things you like in your life and the things you don't like. List what most brings you balance and peace, as well as what most ruins your balance and peace.

Complete this assignment now. Continue reading when finished.

Power Plan

A Power Plan is a vital instrument used while practicing Buddhist mysticism. It is a precise mystical description of your life. Your Power Plan is your unique map to greater personal power, awareness, happiness, and Enlightenment.

Your Power Plan will enable you to clearly see where you are losing energy in your life. Your Power Plan will show you the way to increase your personal power and evolutionary rate. It will give you a measurable structure to advance your spirit.

The first step in developing your Power Plan is to assess your thoughts, activities, and relationships in order to measure their positive and negative impacts on your life. Once you are aware of their implications, it will become clear to you what is positive for your spirit and what is detrimental to your personal power.

Next, you will put your Power Plan into action. Penny for Your Thoughts (an upcoming assignment) is a practice that uses your Power Plan in your everyday life to lead you to greater personal power. This teaches you that the thoughts you think and the activities you engage in profoundly affect your life and well-being.

The Power Plan will help you create antidotes to your own poisonous thoughts and give you shields to defend against harmful situations and people. By executing the Power Plan you will strengthen your mind, find balance, increase your happiness, and expand your awareness.

*

Assignment: Power Plan

We are going to develop your Power Plan by organizing the stories you wrote in previous assignments. What you've uncovered in those teachings is the basis for the Power Plan. The good thing is that you have already done most of the work! Now you're just going to organize and assess it.

Open your Enlightenment Journal to a new page and entitle the page, "Power Plan." List eight column headings in this order:

Upsets
Jealousies
Hurts
-Relationships
General Downs
+Relationships
General Ups
Wonderfuls

Example:

POWER PLAN

Column Headings

Upsets	Jealousies	Hurts	- Relationships	General Downs	+ Relationships	General Ups	Wonderfuls

Now, to develop your Power Plan, review the stories that you've written in the Enlightenment Journal. Categorize them into the above columns. Then you will rate them to determine their negative or positive impacts on your life.

168

Turn to the section of your Enlightenment Journal entitled "Upsets." For each story in the upsets section, come up with a title, a word or a phrase which best describes it. Write the title above or next to the story in your Enlightenment Journal.

After entitling each story in the Enlightenment Journal, enter all the titles in the "Upsets" column of your Power Plan. Next to each title, add a rating. The rating will describe on a scale of 1 through 10 (1 being slightly upset and 10 being extremely upset) how the situation makes you feel.

Example:

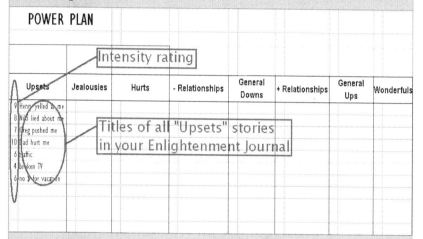

POWER PLAN

Intensity rating

Upsets	Jealousies	Hurts	- Relationships	General Downs	+ Relationships	General Ups	Wonderfuls
9 Henry yelled at me							
8 Nick lied about me							
7 Greg pushed me							
10 Dad hurt me							
6 traffic							
4 broken TV							
6 no $ for vacation							

Titles of all "Upsets" stories in your Enlightenment Journal

Next, develop the "Jealousies" column of your Power Plan in the same way. Turn to the section of your Enlightenment Journal entitled "Inspirations." Title each story. List the titles under the "Jealousies" column of your Power Plan. Rate each entry from 1 to 10 (1 being slightly jealous and 10 being extremely jealous).

Continue by developing the "Hurts" column of your Power Plan in the same way. Turn to the section of your Enlightenment Journal entitled "Rewriting the Past." Title each story. List all the titles under the "Hurts" column of your Power Plan. Rate each entry from 1 to 10 (1 being slightly hurt, and 10 being extremely hurt).

Next, you are going to develop the "-Relationships" column of your Power Plan in the same way. Turn to the section of your Enlightenment Journal entitled "The Power of My Relationships." Add each entry under "Relationships That Decrease My Power" to the "-Relationships" column of your Power Plan. Rate each entry from 1 to 10 (1 being slightly decreasing and 10 being extremely decreasing).

Lastly, you are going to develop the "General Downs" column of your Power Plan in the same way. Turn to the section of your Enlightenment Journal entitled "Things That Affect My Power." Add each entry under "Things That Decrease My Power" to the "General Downs" column of your Power Plan. Rate each entry from 1 to 10 (1 being slightly decreasing and 10 being extremely decreasing).

You have completed an organization and assessment of all of the disempowering conditions of your life. Now you will restate the shields that you had learned in previous assignments for "Upsets," "Jealousies," and "Hurts" in your Power Plan. "-Relationships" and "General Downs" don't have specific shields, but you can use the other shields to moderate many of their effects. "-Relationships" and "General Downs" will use antidotes that you will develop in the next assignment.

To add your shields to the Power Plan, do the following:

Above the "Upsets" column on your Power Plan, write these words: "Shield: I forgive."

Above the "Jealousies" column on your Power Plan, write these words: "Shield: You inspire me!"

Above the "Hurts" column on your Power Plan, write these words: "Shield: Om. The past is dust!"

170

Example:

POWER PLAN

Shield: I forgive.	Shield: You inspire me!	Shield: Om. The past dust!					
Upsets	Jealousies	Hurts	- Relationships	General Downs	+ Relationships	General Ups	Wonderfuls
9 Henry yelled at me	7 Tony's car	10 Sally left me	7 arguing with brother	7 the mall			
8 Niki lied about me	5 Suzy like Tom	6 Henry yelled at me	10 arguing with father	5 taking the bus			
7 Greg pushed me	10 fun musicians	5 Niki lied about me	8 dating Cindy	8 watching tv			
10 Dad hurt me		10 Dad hurt me	5 John	4 feeling sorry			
6 traffic			10 Kate	7 I can't say no			
4 broken TV			7 drinking with Jim	3 presentations			
6 no $ for vacation				6 deadlines			
				10 paying bills			
				3 being bored			
				6 getting ready			
				5 can't sleep			

Now, you are going to develop all of the positive columns of the Power Plan! First, you are going to develop the "+Relationships" column of your Power Plan. Turn to the section of your Enlightenment Journal entitled "The Power of My Relationships." Add each entry under "Relationships That Increase My Power" to the "+Relationships" column of your Power Plan. Rate each entry from 1 to 10 (1 being slightly increasing and 10 being extremely increasing).

Next, you are going to develop the "General Ups" column of your Power Plan in the same way. Turn to the section of your Enlightenment Journal entitled "Things That Affect My Power." Add each entry under "Things That Increase My Power" to the "General Ups" column of your Power Plan. Rate each entry from 1 to 10 (1 being slightly increasing and 10 being extremely increasing).

Write down your highest moments too. What were the highest moments in your life? What experiences were the most awakening, unifying, fun, and Enlightening? List a name or short description for your highest moments in the "Wonderfuls" column.

Come up with wonderful things that are most excellent, noble, and pure! Give each entry a 1 through 10 rating (10 being the best) for how good the entry makes you feel. You should shoot for all 10's!

Now your Power Plan is complete! Here is an example of a complete Power Plan:

POWER PLAN

Shield: I forgive.	Shield: You inspire me!	Shield: Om. The past dust!					
Upsets	Jealousies	Hurts	- Relationships	General Downs	+ Relationships	General Ups	Wonderfuls
9 Henry yelled at me	7 Tony's car	10 Sally left me	7 arguing with brother	7 the mall	9 math teacher	10 mediation	10 scotty dog
8 Niki lied about me	5 Suzy like Tom	6 Henry yelled at me	10 arguing with father	5 taking the bus	8 Jane	9 exercise	10 the beach
7 Greg pushed me	10 fun musicians	5 Niki lied about me	8 dating Cindy	8 watching tv	8 Alex	5 learning math	10 vacations
10 Dad hurt me		10 Dad hurt me	5 John	4 feeling sorry	7 Ron	8 nature	
6 traffic			10 Kate	7 I can't say no	10 Todd	6 flossing	
4 broken TV			7 drinking with Jim	3 presentations		7 dressing well	
6 no $ for vacation				6 deadlines		7 smiling	
				10 paying bills		9 selfless giving	
				3 being bored			
				6 getting ready			
				5 can't sleep			

Your Power Plan shows the conditions of your life. It clearly shows the path to happiness and power. Sun Tzu, the author of *The Art of War*, would say that you have properly conducted a strategic assessment and have properly estimated the conditions of your victory.

Sun Tzu says, "Know yourself and know your enemy, in one thousand battles you will never fail." You know yourself, your higher thoughts and influences that increase your power and happiness. You know your enemy, your lower thoughts and influences that decrease your power and happiness. Now with some effort, victory will be yours.

Assignment: Antidotes

Begin this assignment by looking at yourself in a mirror.

Now that you have categorized, weighted, and estimated all of the conditions of power in your life, state your intention to yourself. To do this, entitle a new page in your Enlightenment Journal, "Antidotes." Take each entry on your Power Plan and write a statement to yourself in definite terms, describing what you intend to do with regard to each entry under each column. Take your time to determine the most constructive way to work with each item on your Power Plan.

Write such statements as:

"I will stop gossiping about other people when I talk to Michael."
"I forgive Henry and will only think of the good things he's done."
"I will stop overeating when I feel nervous."
"I understand that Tom hurt me because he was angry."
"I will no longer be obedient."
"I will spend more time studying computer science."
"I will practice meditation everyday."

Next, look yourself in the eyes in a mirror. Speak your prepared intentions.

Complete this assignment now. Continue reading when finished.

Penny for Your Thoughts

Penny for Your Thoughts is a moment-by-moment practice to exercise mindfulness. Penny for Your Thoughts is a fun game you can play every day. Throughout the day, pay attention to the thoughts you think, the emotions you feel, your reactions, and so on. To play, you will use your Power Plan as a strategic model. You will also keep a daily log called a Power Log to track mindfulness activity.

When something negative comes along, rather than reacting, engaging, or indulging in that negativity, consciously stop yourself. Stop yourself from engaging in any negative action, speech, thoughts, or feelings.

Use the strength of your mind just as you do when you meditate and are mindful. The strength of noticing negativity, letting go of it, and remaining balanced is something you gain with effort in meditation and mindfulness.

Your meditation practice strengthens your mindfulness practice. Your mindfulness practice strengthens your meditation practice. Your success with both practices can be measured over time from the results of the Penny for Your Thoughts exercise.

If your mind is not yet strong enough to stop a thought stream from taking form, as soon as you become aware that you're thinking, feeling, or reacting negatively, use your shields and antidotes!

Your shields are written at the top of the leftmost columns of your Power Plan.

Your shield for Upsets is "I forgive."
Your shield for Jealousies is "You inspire me!"
Your shield for Hurts is "Om. The past is dust!"
Repeat the shield sayings three times.

If your shields fail and your mind becomes poisoned with darkness and negativity, use your antidotes. Antidotes are also used for "-Relationships" and "General Downs." Open your Enlightenment Journal to the section entitled "Antidotes." Find the antidote to what afflicts your mind. Say the antidote three times.

You may also use the substitution technique to aid your mindfulness in Penny for Your Thoughts. With substitution, when you become aware that you're thinking, feeling, or reacting negatively, move your mind to something positive and wonderful.

If you have a negative thought, replace it with a very positive thought from the Wonderfuls column in your Power Plan. For example, if your boss wants to see you in his office and the anxiety that you feel in this situation is rated as a 9 in the General Downs column of your Power Plan, as soon as you start to feel the beginnings of anxiety, you should open your Power Plan and look at the entries in the Wonderfuls column. Seeing the first or second wonderful thing will start a new thought and feeling pattern in your mind and body. Your anxiety will become distant and you will be able to feel more comfortable and balanced when you meet with your boss.

Mindfulness is all about being positive! You'll find that when you engage in activities and relationships that are in the "increase" columns of your Power Plan, you'll naturally have more positive thoughts. The best way to be positive is to make sure that you're not being negative!

A Zen monk had a plant that was a bit neglected. It was a tattered but large plant with several stems and dozens of leaves. The overall appearance of the plant was dreary. A couple of the stems were yellow and drooping. One of the stems was completely brown and dead. Almost a third of the leaves on the plant were wilted or dead. The plant wasn't very happy.

One day the Zen master walked over to the monk's potted plant. Seeing its condition, he plucked the dead stem. Then the Zen master pulled the yellow withering stems. They were not yet dead, but were dying. It was more difficult for the Zen master to pull them out, because the plant was trying to hang on to the life that was left in the dying stems.

Pulling out the dead and dying stems reduced the number of yellow and brown leaves on the plant. Then the Zen master began scrutinizing and pulling dead, withering, and dying leaves from the plant. He evaluated each leaf. If the leaf was soon to die or dead, he plucked it. If the leaf could be recovered, he left it.

After he was done, the plant was smaller, a little bit disheveled looking but had only three or four yellowish leaves amongst the remaining healthy leaves. In a short time, the few leaves that were left wilting and dying grew to be green and bright. The plant grew taller and greener. The plant sprung new stems and new leaves.

When the student asked the Zen master, "How did you miraculously heal this plant?"

The Zen master said, "I didn't. The plant, like all life, flourishes on its own. All I did was pluck away the dying stems and leaves that the plant was giving energy to. When the plant stopped giving energy to its dying parts it flourished on its own accord."

From that day on the student observed the plant and pruned it of any dying leaves or stems. The once withering plant now grew large and beautiful. Over time, through this observance of tending to the plant, the student learned the nature of mind.

Eliminating negative thoughts and emotions from your mind is a continuous exercise. Penny for Your Thoughts is a practice for forming good habits of thought. When you get into the habit of pruning your mind of negativity, eventually you break the karmic chains of dark thoughts and you become habitually positive and happy.

In much the same way that you need to exercise your physical body in order to maintain health and become stronger, you must exercise your mind to maintain balance and become happier. The mind is like a muscle, you have to work it out in order to keep it fit! Penny for Your Thoughts is a workout!

Just as balance is difficult to gain at first in beautiful physical forms such as ballet, balance is also challenging to master in Penny for Your Thoughts. However, keep at it; in every moment you gain more mastery! A balanced mind is like a beautiful dance.

Assignment: Balance

The balance of the mind is similar to physical balance. When you were a baby, it was really hard for you to learn to walk, but after some time, you mastered it and now can walk without thinking about it. Learning balance takes sense and effort for the physical body and for the mind.

Try this:
Stand on one leg.
Lift the knee of the other leg.
Clasp your hands around the knee and hold it up.
Try to stand for 2 minutes.

If you cannot safely do this, modify the exercise so that you can challenge your balance safely.

You'll notice that many muscles in your standing leg work to keep you up. This is how Penny for Your Thoughts works for you mind.

No matter how precarious your situation, many checks and balances and controls of thought keep your state of mind and awareness balanced.

Until you master Penny for Your Thoughts, you'll fall a lot. Falling is OK too. You learn a lot by falling.

Keep working on it and you will not fall again.

Complete this assignment now. Continue reading when finished.

Assignment: Penny for Your Thoughts

In your Enlightenment Journal, start a daily Power Log. Use the Power Log to keep track of any thoughts, feelings, and experiences that match the entries in your Power Plan.

To begin your Power Log, each morning open to a new page in your Enlightenment Journal. At the top center of the page, write the date. Throughout the day, note in your Power Log each occurrence that matches the entries listed in your Power Plan.

Write the entry name from your Power Plan to your Power Log when the thought occurs. If the thought occurs again, simply put a check next to the entry name.

A daily Power Log may look like this:

POWER PLAN

Shield: I forgive.	Shield: You inspire me!	Shield: Om. The past dust!
Upsets	**Jealousies**	**Hurts**
Henry yelled at me	7 Tony's car	10 Sally left me
8 Niki lied about me	5 Suzy like Tom	6 Henry yelled at me
7 Greg pushed me	10 fun musicians	5 Niki lied about me
10 Dad hurt me		10 Dad hurt me
6 traffic		
broken TV		
no $ for vacation		

10/10/2010

POWER LOG

Sally left me	✔	✔	✔	✔
Henry yelled at me (Hurt)	✔	✔	✔	
Henry yelled at me (Upset)	✔	✔		
fun musicians				
broken TV	✔	✔	✔	
no $ for vacation				

Do this exercise religiously for 48 days. Don't just do it, do it all the way. Now that you have become aware of the dark habits of your mind and have intended to do away with them, pull them out by the roots! Watch your mind for 48 days. Practice Penny for Your Thoughts; it will change your life!

Often times while practicing Penny for Your Thoughts you discover many additional negative thoughts and feelings that were overlooked during your initial assessment. If any new thoughts or feelings emerge that are negative to your power and happiness, add them to your Power Plan and give them a rating.

You may also discover some additional thoughts that give you happiness and power. Positive thoughts should be added and rated in your Power Plan as well.

Newly discovered Hurts, Upsets, Jealousies, General Downs, General Ups, Wonderfuls, or new relationships all should be addressed by following the appropriate assignment directions for the category and added and rated in your Power Plan.

For example, if during your first few days of practicing Penny for Your Thoughts, you realize that you have some jealousy and resentment toward your sister because she always wins trophies in tennis, you should make a new entry in your Enlightenment Journal called "New Inspiration" following all of the instructions for the Inspirations assignment. Then you should add this entry to the Jealousies column of your Power Plan and rate it.

You should also make another new entry in your Enlightenment Journal called "New Upset" since this feeling contains both jealousy and resentment. Follow all of the instructions for the Upsets assignment. Then you should add this entry to the Upsets column of your Power Plan and rate it.

For the entire period of this practice you will account for every significant or repeating thought, feeling, relationship, and experience in your Power Log and within the framework of the Power Plan through the reflection of the assignments.

At the end of each day, you will tally and score the negative thoughts that occurred for that day. The logged entries from the Upsets, Jealousies, Hurts, and -Relationships columns of your Power Plan should be included in the tally. This will give you your daily Power Score.

To calculate your Power Score:

1. Open today's Power Log.
2. Identify all of the negative entries.
3. Tally the number of times each entry occurred. For example, "Sally left me" has four checkmarks. That means that you thought "Sally left me" five times on this day. List the number five next to the entry in your Power Log.

10/10/2010

POWER LOG					Total Occurrences
Sally left me	✔	✔	✔	✔	5
Henry yelled at me (Hurt)	✔	✔	✔		4
Henry yelled at me (Upset)	✔	✔			3
fun musicians					1
broken TV	✔	✔	✔		4
no $ for vacation					3

4. Next, refer to your Power Plan and find the rating for each negative thought. Multiply this rating by the number of times it occurred and log this amount.

10/10/2010

POWER LOG					Total Occurrences	Rating Value		Individual Score
Sally left me	✔	✔	✔	✔	5	x 10	=	50
Henry yelled at me (Hurt)	✔	✔	✔		4	x 6	=	24
Henry yelled at me (Upset)	✔	✔			3	x 9	=	27
fun musicians					1	x 10	=	10
broken TV	✔	✔	✔		4	x 4	=	16
no $ for vacation					3	x 6	=	18

5. Determine your daily power score by adding the individual scores together.

10/10/2010 POWER LOG					Total Occurrences		Rating Value		Individual Score	
Sally left me	✔	✔	✔	✔	5	x	10	=	50	
Henry yelled at me (Hurt)	✔	✔	✔		4	x	6	=	24	
Henry yelled at me (Upset)	✔	✔			3	x	9	=	27	
fun musicians					1	x	10	=	10	Sum
broken TV	✔	✔	✔		4	x	4	=	16	
no $ for vacation					3	x	6	=	18	
							Power Score:		$1.45	

As the exercise is called Penny for Your Thoughts, your Power Score is always expressed in pennies. In this example, because the individual scores add up to 145 the Power Score is $1.45.

Every evening, after you've determined your Power Score, you should put this amount of money into your Enlightenment Jar. An Enlightenment Jar is a large jar, tin, or other container that will hold all of your Power Score money for the entire Penny for Your Thoughts exercise. Keep your Enlightenment Jar in a safe place and don't spend the money in it until after completing the exercise.

Write your Power Score in the top right hand corner of your Power Log next to the date.

Now in the same way, tally the Power Log entry totals of the +Relationships, General Ups, and Wonderfuls columns from your Power Plan. This will give your Positive Power Score. Write your Positive Power Score in the top right hand corner of your Power Log under your Power Score. The Positive Power Score gives you important information about how much positive mental and emotional activity was in your attention during the day.

Now subtract your Positive Power Score from your Power Score to give you the Personal Power Score. Write your Personal Power Score in the top right hand corner of your Power Log under your Positive Power Score. Your Personal Power Score let's you know all in all how well you did in personal power on that day.

Penny for Your Thoughts is a demanding practice, but it yields a profound realization! When you earnestly do this exercise you will observe the following results:

1. The first week is the most difficult week of this mindfulness practice. Yet if you do the exercises properly and carefully you will have established a habit of success for the days to come.

2. Up till around day 10 you'll be putting loads of cash into your Enlightenment Jar! The first 10 days are where you are still discovering new Hurts, Upsets, and General Downs to add to your Power Plan.

3. After about day 14 you will really start to see your Power Score dropping and your Positive Power Score rising.

4. Around day 21 you will have the realization of power in your life. This cannot be described, only experienced.

5. Around day 27 you will be able to dispel any dark thoughts from your mind. You will need to work on consistency and being mindful before negative thoughts take hold. You will be scoring close to a zero for your Personal Power Score.

6. Around day 40 you will have become competent at Penny for Your Thoughts. Your Positive Power Score will be high and your Power Score will be low.

7. Around the end of the exercise at day 48 you will have a habitual Power Score of no pennies and a new lease on life!

Continue reading the Enlightenment Workbook. Do the Penny for Your Thoughts assignment in parallel with the next assignments.

Ordering the Chaos of the Mind

Order in your physical life is essential in Buddhist mysticism. Success in spirituality is a balance between the physical world and the nonphysical world. Success is balance.

You seek spiritual experiences in the nonphysical world because you sense the imbalance of an awareness that is too stuck in the physical world. However, it is necessary also to be rooted in the physical world as you study mysticism and explore nonphysical dimensions.

Spiritual seekers in the West often disregard balance, because they just want spiritual experience. Sometimes they are so tired of the physical extreme, they seek a spiritual extreme. These practitioners often seem spaced out and a little weird to normal people in society. Though they have spiritual experiences, they also lack balance. They have gone from too tight to too loose. Lacking balance, their spiritual experiences are akin to the experiences of taking drugs. These kinds of experiences make you feel good for a while and give you altered perceptions of reality, but lack structure and balance. So ultimately these are experiences that do not serve spiritual development.

Balance affords you spiritual experiences that can be integrated into your physical attention. Balanced practice aids the development of spiritual and physical awareness. Balanced spiritual practitioners will see improvement in their physical lives as they practice. They will see improvement in health and fitness. They will see improvement in relating to others. They will see improvement in their financial outlook and career success.

Consider the Buddhist monks of the Far East. Society does not think that they are weird, strange, or odd in any way. Monks are considered to be wise, pure, and holy.

Buddhists in the Far East are not spacey. Buddhist monks are very grounded in their physical reality. Much of what they do throughout the day involves cleaning, cooking, running errands, yard work, and other chores. Buddhist monks must be very disciplined in the physical world so that their practices of spirituality are balanced and successful.

Balance is the middle path. The Buddha at the moment of his Enlightenment described this balance through a gesture. Merged with Nirvana, with his left hand he reached down and touched the ground. The connection of Nirvana and the physical world is Enlightenment.

Assignment: Clean Meditation

As you begin to practice Penny for Your Thoughts, you must strengthen your attention of the physical world so that you can most effectively measure and observe the intangible world of your mind.

You can do this by cleaning house! Clean your room. A cluttered physical life adds clutter to the mind. Cleaning your room enhances your happiness! Cleaning your room enhances your meditation.

Meditate prior to cleaning your room. On a new page in your Enlightenment Journal entitled "Messy Meditation," make an entry describing your meditation experience prior to cleaning your room.

After meditating, clean and organize your room. Clean out your closets. Wash your walls and windows. Throw away garbage. Get rid of the things that you no longer need or use. This adds to a tight and bright life. Make an Enlightenment Journal entry about your meditation experience on a new page in your Enlightenment Journal entitled "Clean Meditation."

Observe your Power Score prior to cleaning, during cleaning, and after cleaning. Did cleaning your room give you power?

Complete this assignment now. Continue reading when finished.

Mystical Fashion

On one occasion at a public meditation seminar, a woman approached her Buddhist teacher with a question. "Can you help me end my depression?" she asked. "I feel bad about myself. I can't think of a reason for my sadness. I just end every day in tears!"

Her teacher nodded and said, "Your mind is conditioned by habitually depressing thoughts, though you lack awareness of them. Meditation is the principal method for ending the karmic chain of thoughts that produce your depression and suffering." He gestured for her to meditate with him. They sat in stillness for several minutes. After the meditation session they bowed.

"That was amazing! I simply disappeared in light!" the woman exclaimed.

"And who was there to be depressed?" her teacher asked.

"No one," she realized.

Her teacher nodded, "There's also a mystical practice that can help you end your habit of depressing thoughts. Would you like to learn about it?"

"Certainly," she said.

"I notice you wear a lot of black clothing," her teacher remarked.

"Yeah, most of my clothes are black. I think black clothing is cool and I like the way it looks on me," she said.

Her teacher nodded and said, "Try this: For a period of one month, wear only brightly colored clothing. As easily as you can learn to be comfortable and happy in different clothing, you can learn to be comfortable and happy with different thoughts. Taking a physical action to change something that is as habitual as your dress style, along with your daily meditation practice will rapidly transform you from a person who is depressed and wears black to a person with positive thoughts and pink sweaters. You'll learn that you can change the addictive habits of mind that have created your sorrows as easily as changing your clothes. Happiness is the new black!"

With diligent practice and pink sweaters for one month, she found that she had no more tears at the end of her days.

Assignment: Dress for Power

Dress differently for a week. Dress a bit more formally. Take the formality of your attire up a notch. Formal dress is always nice and respectable. Dressing more formally is a good idea because in polite society, more formal adornment reflects positively on our character.

Use different colors and styles than you would normally wear. Don't dress in a way that makes you unhappy. Dress in a way that is more formal, fun, and that makes you feel good.

Buy something new. If you're a guy, perhaps buy a new tie. Buy a power tie! Buy a tie that you could wear to an interview. Look at businessmen and politicians to determine what a power tie is.

If you're a gal, perhaps buy a pair of new shoes. Buy a pair of shoes so perfect and so cute that the first thing your girlfriends say when they see you wearing them is, "Those are the cutest shoes!"

What you buy is not mandatory; just buy something that is different and formal for your attire. You can buy anything from a watch to a belt, from earrings to a scarf, from a hat to stockings. Whatever you buy, it must be a replacement for something you already have. So if you buy a pair of formal stockings, you will toss out an old pair of stockings. This article of clothing is not to add clutter to your life but to change your life.

This creates a small but measurable change. If you want to continue to grow, every month buy one new article of clothing that is both more formal and different in color and style than you'd normally wear. Replace an old article of clothing with the new one.

On the seventh day of your dressing adventure, you should wear your new article of clothing with a suit or the most formal attire that you have. Go to a location where others are dressed in suits, perhaps downtown in the business district. Spend at least an hour observing the perception others have of formal dress.

Enter a daily account of your experiences in your Enlightenment Journal on a new page entitled, "Dress for Power."

Observe your Power Score during this assignment. Does changing your attire give you power?

Complete this assignment now. Continue reading when finished.

Assignment: Reflections on Happiness

Now that you are working on monitoring and decreasing the things that take your power away, let's remove a barrier to exploring new things that can give you power and happiness. We'll do this by dispelling the myth that stuff-ism determines your happiness.

Most people engage in stuff-ism and most people just aren't that happy. When you walk down the street and look at people, which of them are happy? Money doesn't make rich people happy. And the lack of money sure doesn't make poor people happy. Relationships don't really seem to fulfill people.

Here's the truth: When people are happy they smile! Go around town and check to see what conditions of stuff-ism make people happy. Many of us think enough money will make us happy.

Entitle a new page in your Enlightenment Journal, "Reflections on Happiness."

Go to McDonald's. See who is smiling.
Go to a fancy restaurant. See who is smiling.
Count the smiles and log them in your Enlightenment Journal.

Look at the drivers of ten old, busted, cheap cars. See who is smiling.
Look at the drivers of ten new, very expensive cars. See who is smiling.
Count the smiles and log them in your Enlightenment Journal.

Many of us think the perfect intimate relationship will make us happy.
Look at ten couples both young and old. See who is smiling.
Count the smiles and log them in your Enlightenment Journal.

Complete this assignment now. Continue reading when finished.

Assignment: Happy Days

What makes you happy? As you practice Penny for Your Thoughts you reduce the negative thoughts and feelings that had been habitual to your awareness. Now begin a new habit of awareness, a habit of happiness.

Be happy for seven days. This will complement your Penny for Your Thoughts assignment. For one week starting today, try to be happy. Even if you're not happy, try to be happy. Happiness is a choice you make!

Your efforts toward happiness should be healthy, constructive, and conducive to Enlightenment. Just give it a shot. Study happiness. Study your happiness. Spend time with the happiest people in your life. Do the things that make you the happiest!

Enter a daily account of your experience in your Enlightenment Journal on a new page entitled, "Happy Days."

Observe how your efforts to be happy change your Power Score. How much of an increase in your Positive Power Score do you see?

Continue with the Enlightenment Workbook while completing this assignment.

Assignment: The Art of Smiling

Spend three days interfacing with people with a genuine smile and an affirming nod. Doing physical things like this can make you happy. When you smile you inspire happiness in yourself! Smiling also inspires happiness in others.

Smiling is a compliment of attention. Pay everyone a compliment! A nod is an affirmation. Nodding tells people that you agree with them, that you accept and affirm who they are. Give everyone an affirming nod!

Now, it's not that you have to have a bobbing head and silly grin on your face all day. Rather you should genuinely smile when interacting with people. When you are genuine, you listen and pay attention to the people you interact with. When you are genuine, your smile comes at the right time and means something to the people you interact with, and it brightens up their day! Your nod should also be genuine, affirming even the smallest positive intention, expression, or act of service.

For example, recently I went to the post office to mail a package. I waited in a long line. When I reached the postal clerk, I could see that she was having a tough time busy with so many people. "Good afternoon, can I help you sir?" she asked in a monotone, routine manner.

I smiled, nodded, and answered, "Good afternoon, yes! I need to send this package." As she helped me, my smile remained. As she affixed the postage to my package, I nodded. As she handed me the receipt for purchase, I nodded.

Then she cracked a smile and said, "Sure has been a long day!" I smiled and nodded.

It's not a big deal right? Smiling and nodding is simply the power to give another a brighter moment from your genuine compliment of attention and affirmation of them.

Enter a daily account of your experience in your Enlightenment Journal on a new page entitled, "The Art of Smiling."

Observe how your efforts to smile and nod change your Power Score. How much of an increase in your Positive Power Score do you see? Does smiling and nodding give you power?

Continue with the Enlightenment Workbook while completing this assignment.

Mystical Exercises

Once at a public meditation seminar, a woman approached her Buddhist teacher asking, "How can I improve my meditation? I feel tired and fatigued every time I sit down to meditate. I feel anxious and can't still my thoughts. It's also very painful for me to sit still for more than five minutes. My back starts hurting. Is there a way that I can improve my practice with these conditions?"

"Yes, of course!" her teacher answered. "You can certainly improve your meditation practice by starting a new cardiovascular exercise program!"

"Exercise program?" the woman questioned. "I do practice yoga. I enjoy stretching and calisthenics more than running. But why should I do physical exercise to improve meditation?"

Her teacher answered, "Exercise is good for everyone. It's part of a healthy lifestyle. But for practitioners of Buddhist mysticism, it's particularly important! When you learned about chakra meditation you learned a little about the aura, your subtle physical energy body that surrounds and encompasses the physical body. You also learned some of the basic structures and relationships of the energetic pathways and energy centers of the aura. As well you learned about the energies that travel along those pathways and to those centers."

Her teacher continued, "During the day the aura gets dirty. The thoughts and impressions of others collect like rubbish in our energy body. This build up of energetic trash can weigh down on our energy body and stagnate and congest the flow of energy within our aura. When your aura is filled with dirty impressions from the intensities of others, you'll start to feel that you have less energy. You may feel sluggish and tired. You may feel unable to concentrate and unable to take on bright tasks or even bright thoughts.

"Certain activities can leave very toxic impressions in your aura that may be very difficult to remove. Toxic impressions can be picked up from engaging in or being subjected to mental or emotional negativity, having sex, healing sick people with toxic auras, spending time in places of negative energy, or doing drugs.

"To keep our energy bodies clean and healthy, we do the exact same thing we need to do to keep our physical bodies healthy. We exercise! Exercising keeps the affected layer of our auras clean from the impressions of others. Exercising for a long enough time burns out the foreign toxicities and impressions in our auras. The reason that I recommend exercise so much for you is that from sex and being exposed to negative people, you have picked up a tremendous amount of toxicity in your aura."

The woman responded, "But I do exercise! I do Hatha yoga every day! I work out at the yoga studio near my house five days a week and I use a self paced yoga video to train on the other days."

Her teacher answered, "Hatha Yoga is good. It's very healthy for some very significant dimensions of your energy body. Tai Chi and Qi Gong are also excellent for important aspects of your aura. But there are many layers of your energy body. In these degrading times and with social conditions as they are in the West, a different layer of our aura is affected more than in other times. Yoga and Tai Chi are exercises that are excellent for layers of your aura that are related to the internal organs, blood, bones, muscles, and tissues. Yoga and Tai Chi are often described as curative for many illnesses of the body."

Her teacher continued, "At a more surface layer of our auras, toxic impressions of others and the overall heaviness of the world affect the balance of our energy. This imbalance serves to create excessive mind activity, anxiety, confusion, and emotional turbulence. To address the health of this level of our auras, cardiovascular exercise heals and purifies these subtle physical structures. It is necessary to keep your heart rate up during a period of exercise for at least 45 minutes to begin to burn away the toxicities in your aura. I recommend at least an hour of exercise per day for subtle physical fitness. When your aura is clean and healthy, it's easier to meditate, see the truth, and let go of addictive habits."

The woman thanked her teacher and agreed to start a cardiovascular exercise program. This information, along with her physical exercise, completely relieved her of anxiety, fatigue, and pain. Her meditation practice bloomed.

Assignment: Exercise Your Aura

Exercise and push yourself a little harder than usual. At a minimum you should do a cardiovascular workout for 45 minutes. If you are accustomed to a longer workout you should try to push your routine about 10% harder and longer. So for example, if you regularly jog 2 miles a day in 60 minutes, try to push your workout to 2.2 miles in 66 minutes. If you are comfortable pushing it harder, push it harder! The goal is to work out as hard as you can without injuring yourself and still be able to work out the next day.

Do this assignment safely. If you do not currently have an exercise routine, slowly work your way up to the 45 minute minimum. Perhaps go running for 15 to 20 minutes a day for a week, then increment your workout time by five minutes every few days until you reach the 45 minute minimum. Whenever starting a new exercise routine, it is always recommended that you consult a physician before beginning.

After pushing yourself to 45 minutes of cardiovascular exercise or 10% beyond your usual cardiovascular exercise routine limits, catch your breath, hydrate, take notice of how you feel, and then meditate. It's nice to take a shower and get out of your exercise clothes, or at least wash your face and hands.

Extended cardiovascular exercise burns impurities and toxicities out of your aura. With a healthier physical and subtle physical body, meditation and happiness are easier.

Entitle a new page in your Enlightenment Journal, "Exercise Your Aura!" and write about your experience.

How did you feel while exercising? How did you feel after exercising? What was your meditation like? Observe how your exercise changes your Power Score. Do you see an increase in your Positive Power Score? Does exercise give you power?

Continue with the Enlightenment Workbook while completing this assignment.

Selfless for Yourself

On another occasion at a public meditation seminar, a middle-aged gentleman approached his Buddhist teacher and said, "Nothing I do makes me happy! I've been looking everywhere for happiness for the past ten years, but I am bored beyond belief with my life! I've bought things to make me happy like sports cars, vacation homes, and Rolex watches, but they didn't fulfill me. I had relationships that were fun, but now I've been divorced twice. I've tried learning new things to make me happy by becoming a helicopter pilot, SCUBA diver, and wine connoisseur! But none of the things I did worked to make me happy. That's why I've come to meditation, to learn how to break free from my discontent."

His teacher nodded understandingly. Then the man asked his teacher, "Is there something that I can do now that will make me happy? Is there a spiritual secret that can free me from the prison of my circumstance?"

Smiling, his teacher said, "There is! There is a fast path out of the dissatisfaction of the self! There is a shortcut to happiness! Would you like to learn it?"

"Yes. I'd be very happy to learn this shortcut to happiness!"

"It's going to be challenging at first! Are you sure you want to learn it?"

"Yes, definitely," he replied. "I'm very intrigued. I want to see if the spiritual shortcut to happiness will work for me!"

"Oh, it will work alright," his teacher said, "but first, before class this evening I heard you giving some advice to a young lady over there regarding her career. What is your occupation?"

"I am a successful computer programmer. I was telling her about the many benefits she could gain if she pursued a career in technology."

"Would you tutor her and a few other students here who are interested in learning technology?" his teacher asked.

"I'm not sure," he replied. "I am very busy these days. I really don't have the time to teach a bunch of kids. I don't think I can really help them anyway." Then he asked, "So what about the shortcut to happiness? That's what I want to learn here!"

"You'll learn all about the shortcut to happiness if you teach these young men and women technology three days per week for one month!" his teacher replied.

"OK, OK," he said in the cool voice of a savvy negotiator. "I'll do this for you, if you'll promise to teach me the shortcut to happiness after."

His teacher smiled and agreed, "It's a deal!"

He spent the next month teaching several of the meditation students about technology. They were very inspired about working in technology after the month of study.

As soon as the month was up, the gentleman again approached his teacher and said, "OK, I've done my part! I've taught Jim, Sue, Mike, and Sarah some cutting edge information technology and how to succeed in a computer programming career." He paused and then said, "Ya know, they are pretty fantastic students! With some practice they'll master programming and have a rewarding career." He paused again and then said, "Oh, I almost forgot! OK, now it's your turn to tell me the shortcut to happiness."

"I already have and you've already taken the shortcut," his teacher replied.

"What do you mean? I don't even know what the shortcut is! You haven't told me anything yet. You made me teach the kids before teaching me the shortcut to happiness."

"Let me ask you," his teacher said, "How do you feel? Do you still feel dissatisfied? Are you still unhappy?"

He thought about it for a moment or two and then replied, "Well no, I don't feel unhappy at all. Maybe it's because I've been so busy teaching the kids. It has been a lot of time-consuming work!"

"Tell me, how did it go with teaching the kids?" his teacher asked.

"It went great!" he replied. "It was a bit of a challenge in the beginning. I had to organize and structure a lesson plan and make homework assignments. We had a lot of fun with the final project! They all have successfully written a working program in this new technology! Actually even though you've only asked me to teach them for one month, I've decided to continue to meet with them on the weekends for the next six months. I believe that they'll need some more support and instruction. Sue is a very smart gal! She's learned so much so quickly! And Mike, though it's a bit challenging for him to learn, he works so hard that it inspires me! I really want to show him that he can master technology!"

"There it is!" his teacher said.

"What?" he asked.

"The shortcut to happiness," his teacher answered.

The man furrowed his brow, perplexed.

His teacher explained, "Last month you told me that the many things you've done in the past ten years to make yourself happy have left you unfulfilled. This is because you've been focusing on fulfilling the wrong person: you! When your focus is your own happiness, the egotism and self-absorption of seeking fulfillment often leads to misery. There is no peace in seeking for the self. All your selfish efforts for happiness have only driven you to boredom, sorrow, and a limited self-description. Rather, follow the spiritual law of the universe: Advance your happiness by advancing the happiness of others. Helping others, focusing on the happiness and well-being of others, is a sure way to become happy yourself. And as you can see from your own experience, it is the shortcut to happiness!"

He smiled and thanked his teacher. The next day he started a new introduction to technology course. Eight students attended. He was happy to help them!

Assignment: Selfless Giving

Go out and do something for someone in need. Go out and do three acts of selfless kindness. Help someone out. Maybe feed the homeless. Perhaps help a friend or relative for nothing in return. Use right intent.

Entitle a new page in your Enlightenment Journal, "Selfless Giving." Write the accounts of your three acts of selfless kindness. What were your feelings about doing each act in the beginning, middle, and at the end?

Observe how your selfless giving changes your Power Score. How much of an increase in your Positive Power Score do you see? Does selfless giving give you power?

Complete this assignment now. Continue reading when finished.

Assignment: A Day in Nature

Spend a day in nature. Go with a friend or go alone. Find the most beautiful place of nature near you. Go to a place where you can hike or sit in solitude. Find a place of nature where you can be secluded from other people.

Meditate, relax, explore, and have fun. Spend at least a few hours in nature. If you are with a friend, give each other some space for self-reflection. It's fine to hike and talk together, but also make sure you have time to meditate and sit alone.

Entitle a new page in your Enlightenment Journal, "A Day in Nature." Write down the reflections, thoughts, and feelings that you had while experiencing a day in nature.

Observe how your day in nature changes your Power Score. How much of an increase in your Positive Power Score do you see? Does a day in nature give you power?

Complete this assignment now. Continue reading when finished.

Conclusion

Now you have experienced the beginning of the pathway to Enlightenment. Now you have opened the doorway to self-knowledge. You have become aware of some of the deeper truths of life. You have started the adventure of self discovery, the pathway to Enlightenment.

You broke through the limited views of the stories you've always believed to reveal greater truth and possibilities. Knowing the limitation and partiality of all stories, you read many mystical stories that guided you along with assignments to discover a complete truth: your story. You have recollected and written your true story, and the story goes on and on forever.

In the beginning you wrote your initial story. The story of yourself, your life, what you believe, and what you've learned. The story that you entitled "The Stories of My Life" illustrated many of the definitions of your consciousness.

Next you studied the story of the Buddha and learned the events of the life of a person who transcended all levels of definition of consciousness and all levels of limited awareness to reach Enlightenment, eternal liberation. Learning the biography of one who succeeded in awakening on the spiritual path shows you the way to liberation in the course of reflection of your own life.

In the great traditions of Enlightenment in ancient India, as well as in Zen and other forms of Buddhism, during meditation, practitioners would focus, still their minds, stop their thoughts, and from the deepest depths of their souls question themselves and the universe with this query: "Who am I?" When the answer is revealed to this "Big Picture" question, Enlightenment is realized.

When first pondering this spiritual question, "Who am I?" what first comes to mind is what you wrote about in your "The Stories of My Life" section of your Enlightenment Journal. These are things that tightly bind consciousness to your views, your experiences, your relations. This is to say that this is your description of the world, all of life squeezed into your incomplete and partial model of reality.

This separatist view was initiated by your ignorance of the unity of all things. Being separate, your fears, desires, and clinging create more and more dualistic views of life and self. These selfish forces and reactions lead to tremendous fragmentation of attention, delusion, and suffering. These selfish forces drive the contraction of awareness and limitation of consciousness.

Later when studying the "Right View" teachings of the Buddha, you were able to expose the limited model of the self by pondering an old photograph of yourself at a young age and asking the "Big Picture" question, "Who am I?" again from a more fluid point of view to discover a deeper, more spiritually true view of self.

Finally you learned to create a mystical description of your self and the world, your Power Plan. You also learned to view your whole life in a mystical way through the awareness of each moment using your Power Log. These mystical techniques show you powerful truths of who you are so that you can swiftly ascend in spiritual awareness in a constructive and measurable manner.

The final truth of who you are is something you will discover for yourself through the realization of unity and the end of the awareness-binding, clinging and grasping ego.

Enlightenment is nothing that you're going to find from reading a book or hearing a teacher speak. What will bring you to Enlightenment is what you've done with this book: Explore what is, understand truth for yourself, and take the side of light and understanding in all endeavors. The next step is up to you.

You have seen beneath the surface of your life. You have learned that there are structures you can stand on. You've assembled your Power Plan and can use it to better your life. Just as you were able to use power to evolve beyond who you thought you were and what you thought you could do by pushing yourself to do ten more pushups in the assignment in your Enlightenment Journal entitled "My Description of Self," you can move beyond all limitation of self! You can free yourself of the past and end limiting karmas. You can focus on positive and wonderful things and transform into a completely new and Enlightened being!

Concluding Assignment

When you've completed 48 days of practicing Penny for Your Thoughts, you have one final assignment. Take the money in your Enlightenment Jar and use it as a selfless giving for others.

The pennies in the Enlightenment Jar are symbols of your un-Enlightenment. Each penny represents un-Enlightened activity. Your un-Enlightened activity has been accounted, collected, and represented as monetary value. Through this powerful act, your un-Enlightenment is transformed in the Enlightened activity of selfless giving.

From the money in your Enlightenment Jar, give the most Enlightening gift you can. Just as food is a physical thing that is transformed into the energy for your life, your pennies and selfless giving transform into Enlightenment.

Please continue on to the next page now.

A True Story

Once, a student approached his teacher seeking answers to his troubles. Raising his index finger before his teacher he said, "First, I'm confused about how to practice and what to do with my life."

"Second," he raised another finger, holding two fingers before his teacher and said, "I don't know if I am any good at all this spiritual stuff anyway. Maybe I was just being too hopeful. I'm not honestly sure if Enlightenment is real or if I can attain it."

"Third," now holding three fingers up, he continued, "My family is all over my case and they need help from me. But I have so much work to do! I'm not even sure if my work is useful or fulfilling anymore, but it demands my time! Even if I do take time off to help my family, I won't be able to bring myself to talk to my father after our last argument. He's impossible!"

Raising his pinky finger in an exacerbated manner, and holding four fingers in front of his teacher, he said, "And I'm messing things up with Sally. She needs my support right now but I have so many pressures on me and confusions that I am really making a mess of things!"

Turning his hand palm up in a questioning gesture, he shook his head feeling overwhelmed. Again reflecting on his life, he clenched his hand into a tight fist and asked, "Who am I? And where is Enlightenment?"

His teacher reached out with both of his hands and gently began to open his clenched fist and said, "This is who you are." The student looked at his fist as it loosened and his fingers unfurled. He gazed at the emptiness of his open palm as his teacher said, "And Enlightenment is here." His teacher lifted his open hand and placed it firmly over his heart.

44716272R00117

Made in the USA
San Bernardino, CA
21 July 2019